Challenges in Forensic Psychotherapy

Forensic Focus

Edited by Murray Cox

This new series takes the currently crystallizing field of Forensic Psychothreapy as its focal point, offering a forum for the presentation of theretical and clinical issues. It also embraces such influencial neighbouring disciplines as language, law, literature, criminology, ethics and philosphy, as well as psychiatry and psychology, its established progenitors.

Forensic Focus 5

Challenges in
Forensic Psychotherapy

Edited by Hjalmar van Marle

Foreword by Murray Cox

Jessica Kingsley Publishers
London and Bristol, Pennsylvania

The right of the contributors to be identified as the authors of this work has been asserted by them in accordance with the Copyright, Designs and Patents Act 1988.

First published in the United Kingdom in 1997 by
Jessica Kingsley Publishers Ltd
116 Pentonville Road
London N1 9JB, England
and
1900 Frost Road, Suite 101
Bristol, PA 19007, U S A

Library of Congress Cataloging in Publication Data
A CIP catalogue record for this book is available from the Library of Congress

British Library Cataloguing in Publication Data
Challenges in forensic psychotherapy. – (Forensic focus;
5)
1. Psychology, Forensic 2. Forensic psychiatry 3. Psychology,
Forensic – Congresses 4. Forensic psychiatry – Congresses
I. Marle, Hjalmar van
616.8'914

ISBN 1-85302-419-8

Printed and Bound in Great Britain by
Athenæum Press, Gateshead, Tyne and Wear

Contents

Part One: Paradigm and Practice

Part Two: Treatment Issues

Part Three: Psychotherapy and the Criminal Justice System

Part Four: The Reality of the Victim

Foreword

Challenges and Forensic Psychotherapy are never far from each other. As this growing realm of professional expertise begins to establish its borders, so it posits challenges to related disciplines. We therefore speak of the challenge *of* Forensic Psychotherapy and yet we daily face challenges *to* Forensic Psycho-therapy from theoretical, practical as well as economic and other executive pressures.

This book conveys the vigour of debate *within* Forensic Psychotherapy itself. To describe it as the 'proceedings' of a formal conference is to miss its vitality. The etymology of process and proceeding (Latin *procedere* – to go forward) invites us to such themes as advance, orderly succession and other ways of referring to forward movement. This book is thus welcome in the Forensic Focus series which focuses on these very things.

Murray Cox
October 1996

Preface

At The Hague Conference of the International Association for Forensic Psychotherapy (IAFP) in 1994 forensic psychotherapists unfolded their views on their discipline and presented their methods of treatment. The conference title: 'Challenges in Forensic Psychotherapy' invited trespass over the boundaries laid by traditional psychotherapy and by the criminal justice system in search of better integration and even synergy between these two constituent parts.

In this book the reader will find strategies of psychodynamic psychotherapy with forensic patients where he perhaps expected to find a supportive stance, and a containing, therapy-oriented criminal justice system instead of a harsh and punitive one. Regulations and laws are here to prepare and to provide opportunities for psychotherapeutic treatment of offenders with personality disorders or a dual diagnosis, for some in combination with medication.

Forensic psychotherapy has developed over the last fifty years from psychotherapy with delinquents on psychoanalytic lines ('searchlights on delinquency') to a interdisciplinary approach which influences and researches not only the individual patient but also the interactions between therapy and setting, the position of the victim, and the major influences of legislation, prison accommodation and staff, and social policy. The IAFP Conference in 1994 provided an excellent reflection on the present state of the art of forensic psychotherapy as the contributions brought together a 'Gestalt' which was consistent and diverse but also produced enough conclusions for new practice and new challenges for research.

Therefore, as editors we are glad that the contributors to that conference have so enthusiastically handed over their presentations and worked together with us to provide this book which without doubt will facilitate further development of theory and applications. The contents reflect the different aspects of the essential subject which is the mentally abnormal offender with his past and present interactions, as a perpetrator and a victim himself, trying to give meaning to his or hers life often by destroying the lives of others, to be detained for the sake of society and him or herself.

The purpose of this volume made clear, we hope that it may find its way to the forensic therapists and decision makers in that field, and that it may serve as an introduction to those who are interested in this complicated matter.

Hjalmar van Marle

PART ONE

Paradigm and Practice

Offenders Who Can and Who Cannot be Treated in the Netherlands

Wilma van den Berg and Hjalmar van Marle

FORENSIC PSYCHOTHERAPY AND THE DUTCH PENAL LAW

In retrospect, the introduction of legislation on psychopathy in the Netherlands in 1925 led to the present richly varied system of ways of treatment, aimed at a great diversity of offenders suffering from all sorts of disturbances. With the introduction of better psychiatric and psychotherapeutic methods and the disappearance from the general psychiatric institutions of those brought to court, the original goal of the so-called TBS (literally 'detention under Government' orders), providing care for mentally disturbed offenders in security institutions, has changed to the treatment of both motivated and non-motivated delinquents in various degrees of freedom. The voluntary character is based on a choice between two evils: agree to treatment or else be locked up in prison.

Although care and treatment under the TBS measure are discussed elsewhere, by way of introduction, in this chapter we will describe the different nature of forensic (psycho)therapeutic treatment of mentally disturbed prisoners in the Dutch prison system. Such treatment is of a special nature because of the circumstances under which it takes place: an environment where punishment is put first and foremost, with fewer (and less skilled) staff than is the case in psychiatric institutions, where vulnerable groups such as sexual delinquents run risks and drug addicts thrust their own subculture upon others. A dominant jail culture exists, with social conventions that are in full contrast with those that exist in the psychotherapeutic discourse. The atmosphere in the room of the therapist may be one hundred per cent different from that in the rest of the penal institution.

In the Dutch penal system there is also a clear distinction between punishment and treatment. In the latter case the attempt is made to manipulate the disturbance in the personality to such a degree that the delinquent will become less dangerous and will not commit another serious crime. This so-called dualist sanctioning system of punishment and coercive measures considers the safeguarding of the society to be the main reason for the coercive measure; the principle reason for punishment is a certain amount of culpability. The basic principle is that only those will be punished who can be held responsible for their behaviour.

The choice between punishment or coercive measure will be determined by the judge, based on the degree of responsibility of the suspect. The basic principle is the mental health of those brought to court (full responsibility). In case of a disorder, the judge will decide on the basis of reports by behavioural experts to what extent this disturbance has influenced the behaviour of the suspect at the moment of the offence.

If a punishable act has been proved and the offender is considered of unsound mind then the Dutch criminal court can sentence him to be sent to a psychiatric hospital for a year. If he is still considered mentally disturbed and dangerous after this year, then he can be detained for an unlimited period of time by making use of the possibilities offered under civil law by authority of the court, till the psychiatrist thinks the risks are acceptable for his return to society.

In the penal framework the TBS measure is a form of coercive treatment which is in principle unlimited in time, and thereby the most drastic form of psychiatric treatment. The danger that due to his disturbance an offender might commit another serious crime must then be so great that only the TBS will offer sufficient protection. The convict will then be forced to stay in a security clinic till in the opinion of the psychiatrist and the judge he is no longer dangerous to society. It is true, that there is always the possibility that he will not be cooperative in his treatment but he will consequently be considered dangerous for society even longer and will have to stay in the hospital longer. No doubt for some this form of motivation is the only reason that they allow themselves to be treated.

Until 1988 there was also the system of the so-called conditional TBS: if a delinquent did not cooperate with either an ambulant treatment or clinical treatment, which the court thought necessary, then a forced treatment in a maximum security institution could be imposed. This used to be a highly useful measure for those who were sentenced but in whose cases doubt remained whether the ultimum remedium of a TBS measure was strictly essential. Unfortunately in 1988 this option disappeared from the law; the so-called

'TBS with instructions' replaced this option. Also this measure aims at getting an offender treated in a less drastic way so that he becomes less dangerous, but there is no sanction when the person involved does not observe the instructions. That is why this form of TBS is hardly used by the judge and is in fact of no value. Meanwhile a bill has been introduced which aims at reintroducing the conditional TBS in a slightly altered version.

Another form of forensic treatment that can be imposed by the judge is of a more voluntary character: one can withdraw from treatment but then a prison sentence will be carried out. If someone is suffering from a mental disorder but the crime is not so serious, and the risk of a relapse is considered to be acceptable, then the judge can give a suspended, conditional sentence, the condition being that person must cooperate with treatment. This treatment can include out patient therapy or in patient therapy in a specific clinic. A prison sentence of a maximum of one year need not be executed if the offender cooperates in the therapy, with a maximum probationary period of three years. For less motivated persons this condition can be decisive in taking the treatment seriously.[1] Details on the success of this form of motivation are not available, though.

MENTALLY DISTURBED OFFENDERS IN PRISON

In the case of diminished responsibility, that is the offence is to some extent determined by a mental disorder, but cannot fully be explained by this disorder, then for the part of the psychological functioning for which there did exist freedom of choice, a prison sentence may follow.

Consequently, offenders suffering from serious disorders can also be placed in penitentiary institutions. On the one hand there is the principle 'no punishment without guilt': anyone who is not responsible at all for his behaviour cannot be sentenced to punishment. On the other hand, following jurisprudence of the highest Dutch Court, 'de Hoge Raad' (the Dutch Supreme Court), punishment to the extent of guilt need not be imposed. If for example somebody committed a crime under the influence of a mental disorder and the judge consequently considers him less responsible, then based on the part relating to what he must be held responsible for, the judge can still sentence him to a long imprisonment.

For in determining the punishment the judge does not only take into consideration the degree of guilt of the offender, but will also include to what extent society is shocked by the offence, the need for a form of redress for the next of kin, the deterrent effect of the punishment and so forth.

---

1   See also below *Between Couch and Bench* in this book.

Sometimes there may also be a mental disorder of the offender (e.g. an eating disorder) but no relation between the disorder and the offence. Then the offender will be held responsible for his behaviour and only a prison sentence will follow. As is evident from the above examples, there may be mentally disturbed inmates in prison without (the expectation of) treatment in a psychiatric department.

Compared to our neighbouring countries, from the 19th century to the mid-1970s of the 20th century, there were not many prisoners in the Netherlands. For a long time the size of the criminal population was relatively small and besides it mainly related to crime against property and hardly included violent crime. In general there was no need for administering high punishments. In the early 1970s there even existed overcapacity and penitentiary institutions were closed.

However, in the 1980s serious crime (especially relating to drugs) increased rapidly, and long prison sentences were imposed. Therefore more prison cells were necessary. The number of prison cells has increased explosively these last two decades, and is still increasing. Around 1984 the total capacity was approximately 4000 cells; ten years later this number had increased to more than 7500. At the end of 1996 there will be more than 13,000 cells available in the Netherlands. The number of cells in the Netherlands will then be somewhat higher than the average number of cells in Europe.[2]

To control the costs of these new penitentiary institutions, the latest policy plans austerity of the day programmes for the prisoners, in which labour as the most important activity is stressed. In practice this will mean that the prisoners will be confined to their cells much longer. This in itself will cause extra mental problems and may lead to more mentally disturbed prisoners.

Since World War II the Dutch prison system has been characterized by a humanitarian tradition. The aim of the Dutch prison system is not only to provide a safe society by temporarily removing lawbreakers from society, but the detention must also be geared to the reintroduction of the prisoners to social life, so-called rehabilitation. This means limiting the harmful effects of the detention, and improving the possibility that after imprisonment, prisoners can play a positive role in social life. In the long run a safe society can be promoted in this way. This means assisting the prisoner with his return to society by creating the conditions for a successful reintegration. Moreover, there is the obligation to provide good care for the prisoner, i.e. promoting the healthy physical and psychological well-being of the prisoners.

---

2   1994 Annual report by the 'Centrale Raad voor de Strafrechtstoepassing' (Central Authority for the Penal Code).

At this very moment in the various Dutch penitentiary institutions there is a growing number of prisoners with serious psychiatric problems, including prisoners with personality disorders. Recent research by the Ministry of Justice proves that 12 per cent of all offenders in security institutions need extra mental care.[3] Apart from the prisoners who are to be held less responsible for their offences, this also relates to prisoners suffering from serious mental disorders as a result of the prison system, their drug history or their coming to terms with the offence.

In view of the obligation to provide care and the aim at rehabilitation, these mentally disturbed persons shall have to be taken care of because (or for the period during which) removal is not possible.

The 'Standard Minimum Rules for the Treatment of Prisoners' adopted by the Council of Europe, which also apply to the Netherlands, includes the obligation to provide psychiatric treatment to prisoners who need it. Article 21 of this rule runs as follows: 'At every institution there shall be available the services of at least one general practitioner. The medical services should be organized in close relation with the general health administration of the community or nation. They shall include a psychiatric service for the diagnosis and, in proper cases, the treatment of states of mental abnormality.'; and article 63 runs: 'The medical services of the institution shall seek to detect and shall treat any physical or mental illnesses or defects which may hamper a prisoner's rehabilitation. All necessary medical, surgical and psychiatric services shall be provided to that end.'[4] This responsibility also applies to those who, whether they are yet convicted or not, find themselves in a crisis as a result of which there will not be any time to prepare their transfer to special facilities.

The largest group of prisoners stays in remand centres: they have a strong feeling of uncertainty about their future. They are only suspected of penal offences and it is unclear whether they will be sentenced to imprisonment or to a TBS, or whether they might be acquitted of the charges. From a legal point of view there is no basis for enforcing psychiatric treatment. Under special legal provision[5] those suffering from very serious mental illnesses can temporarily be placed in psychiatric hospitals or in TBS hospitals.

These facilities often have long waiting-lists or refuse to accept these persons. Also those who were sentenced to imprisonment can if necessary on the basis of legal provisions be detained in a TBS hospital or be placed in a

---

3   Report by the 'deelprojectgroep Psychisch gestoorde gedetineerden' (subprojectgroup prisoners with mental disorders), Project Regime 1st phase, December 1994.

4   Standard Minimum Rules for the Treatment of Prisoners, adopted by the Committee of Ministers on 19 January 1973 at the 217th meeting of the Ministers' Deputies.

5   Article 47 'Gevangenismaatregel' (prison regulation) offers the possibility to temporarily send mentally disturbed prisoners (till they have recovered according to a doctor) to a psychiatric hospital.

psychiatric hospital for the time of their prison sentence.[6] The flow of mentally disturbed persons from penitentiary institutions to general psychiatric hospitals has stagnated for years.

Lack of expertise and capacity to help patients brought to court and their negative image are the causes. However, in these last few years a number of intramural facilities of the mental national health have become more accessible for admission and treatment of those sentenced to imprisonment and suffering from personality disorders.[7] On a voluntary basis, these then are placed in a (psycho)therapeutic treatment institution till the end of their prison sentence. If they do not cooperate with the treatment, they are returned to prison.

To increase the flow from maximum security hospitals, apart from three forensic psychiatric clinics, since 1991 ten beds have been financed in four psychiatric hospitals each, so-called forensic psychiatric units. At this moment there are several requests from other psychiatric hospitals to develop such units.

SPECIAL TREATMENT UNITS IN PRISON

Under the earlier-mentioned dual penal system in the Netherlands, an institution labelled prison or remand centre cannot have the character of a treatment clinic. If the judge imposes a prison sentence, it is evident that the prisoner can be held responsible for his offences and must pay the price by imprisonment. Prisons that function only on the basis of therapeutic principles will consequently lose their retaliatory function.

However, because in the prison system there are disturbed prisoners, and because care for prisoners creates obligations for the state, the environment in special small-scale units in penitentiary institutions is made suitable to carry out, for example, psychotherapy. Eventually, according to policy, every penitentiary institution will have a small unit to provide special care. The psychological care of prisoners will be geared at the individual and his problems as much as possible. If the institution itself cannot provide sufficient care, then replacement must follow. At this moment there are six Individual Care Units (IBA) at a regional level, three for those not yet sentenced in remand centres and three for those found guilty, in prisons.

The IBAs have further options for individualizing the treatment and have more (specialized) staff. An IBA is to be found in a separate section of an

---

6 Article 13 'Wetboek van Strafrecht' (Penal Code) offers the option to send mentally disturbed prisoners to a clinic for those placed under Government's orders, and if necessary even to the end of their prison sentence. Article 47 of the prison regulation can also be applied to prisoners.
7 Sending to a number of specialized institutions under article 47 'Gevangenis-maatregel' Prison regulation ('Groot Batelaar' in Lunteren, 'De Gaarshof' in Baarle Nassau, the Forensic psychiatric clinic 'Licht en Kracht' in Assen and the day treatment clinic of the 'Dr Henri van der Hoeven Kliniek' in Utrecht).

institution and in principle provides 24 places, distributed over two communal units of 12 places each. In the case of IBAs for those not sentenced, it is often a matter of preventing or intervening in a crisis situation, and the individual approach is central. In the case of IBAs for those sentenced a rather groupwise approach is central. The idea is that in the two forms of IBAs, activities will take place along a policy plan on the basis of individual treatment schemes; there always exists a continuing process of observation, reporting and evaluation. There is more staff than in a ordinary unit: four warders for every 24 prisoners instead of two in a regular unit.

Since the early 1990s a psycho-medical team (PMT) has operated in most penitentiary institutions (remand centres and prisons). The goal of the PMT, which includes the institution psychologist, the district psychiatrist, the institution doctor and the nurse, is to coordinate social and therapeutic activities and to gear these to each other. Moreover, warders are advised on the way these prisoners must be supported. For every institution one can differentiate between prisoners who must be handled according to standard policy and prisoners who on the grounds of psychiatric or serious psycho-social problems need special care.

The PMT also has other tasks, including to provide a diagnosis, to coordinate the therapeutic activities between the staff involved, and to meet the agreements as regards the prisoners, to provide direct help to prisoners (crisis intervention, assistance, treatment), consultation, and advising the staff carrying out the immediate work, and asking the support of external experts. Weekly, the PMT discusses the prisoners selected for special care. If necessary they are directed to the regional or national facilities.

If the support in the IBAs is insufficient then there are also facilities on a national level such as Forensic Observation and Care Unit (FOBA) and three Security Individual Care Units (BIBA). The BIBA, which belongs to a remand centre in Amsterdam, has a national function of crisis intervention, especially in case of psychotic prisoners. It offers temporary support after which they are sent back to the institution of origin. The BIBA also functions as a link to external facilities. The BIBAs, separate units in prisons, are meant for disturbed prisoners who are also likely to escape by aggressive means.

The Penitentiary Selection Centre (PSC) also has a national function; this centre possesses a therapy unit for eight prisoners with long prison sentences and suffering from personality disorders, in the last phase (about 18 months) of their detention. To be accepted they must have proved to be sufficiently motivated, to have sufficient ego-strength to be able to more or less stand confrontations with their own functioning, and be able to make use of leave opportunities without society running too many risks. The aim is an integrated treatment, during which by means of sociotherapy and an individual psychotherapy, the treatment target is reached which is defined for every prisoner

(Smits 1994). The PSC also has a unit for clinical psychological research meant for selection and detention support.

There are concrete policy plans to realize more (about ten) regional IBAs. To be recognized as such, the presence of a well-functioning policy-making psychologist, a psycho-medical team to which the psychiatrist contributes substantially and a technically separated unit for at least 24 places is required. This extension is the result of an investigation carried out in 1994 into the number and the problems of disturbed prisoners within the Dutch prison system.[8] The results of the investigation identify those prisoners suffering from mental disorders, especially those who have committed violent crimes (including homicide). The prevalent illnesses are psychosis and affective disorders. About three-quarters of these prisoners suffer also from personality disorders, mainly antisocial, borderline, theatrical, and narcissistic personality disorders. In a number of cases there exists multiple psychiatric illnesses. And in a considerable number of cases, there also exists addiction, suicidal intentions, behavioural problems or transcultural problems. Nearly one-third of the problem group has a clinical psychiatric past. The lack of available places in general psychiatry is in fact one of the causes of the growth of the number of psychotic prisoners. As a result of the decrease of the number of hospital beds and a stricter interpretation of the legal conditions (dangerousness) for forced hospitalization in psychiatry, more and more patients are not admitted or are released too early. Besides, there are the general social factors which as a whole cause criminality to increase. The result of this is also that psychological unstable persons will slip back into criminal behaviour.

METHODS OF TREATMENT

After World War II there were many authorities in the Netherlands who during the German occupation experienced a stay in prisons themselves. During the post-war reconstruction in the Netherlands there existed the drive to offer a more humane approach towards prisoners and those detained in TBS hospitals and, more than before, to use their stay for an active preparation aimed at their rehabilitioń. For the TBS institutions, this especially meant that modern psychiatric treatment methods, as these were developing at that time, were actively accepted and applied. Just as was the case in the entire system of psychiatry then, there existed a feeling of optimism on treatment methods in the TBS institutions and also a positive idea in prisons on the possibilities of resocialization. There too, incidental treatment possibilities were created for those with long prison sentences.

---

8   Report by the 'deelprojectgroep Psychisch gestoorde gedetineerden' (subprojectgroup prisoners with mental disorders), Project Regime 1st phase, December 1994.

Besides the psychiatric treatment framework, psychotherapeutic ways of treatment were also introduced which, with some modification, were adopted from the regular national health system by the TBS institutions and the prisons. At first, in all these institutions there existed psychodynamic, even psychoanalytical treatment philosophies, entirely in line with the professional standard of that time. Later on some differentiation of these concepts about ways of treatment developed into, for example, behavioural therapeutic and group therapeutic principles. At the moment though, as a whole, more attention is given to the dangerousness-predicting behaviour of each individual and psychotherapy now often takes place eclectically: psychoanalytic approaches are used next to cognitive psychotherapeutic and behaviouristic principles.

An essential principle, as is defined in the penal code, remains central in practice, namely a clear cut difference between providing care on the one hand and treatment on the other. Under the Constitution forced treatment is not allowed in the Netherlands. To prevent the risk of recidivism for society the penal code, however, requires a forced stay in an institution, but further treatment is only necessary in case of disorders which provoke severe dangerousness and in case of participation in the rehabilitation process. Providing care does mean accepting mentally disturbed offenders in a security setting adapted to their own needs, and does offer the possibility of not distinguishing beforehand between persons that can or cannot be treated.

It is planned to offer to those placed in TBS hospitals, such a specific setting which is necessary either to prevent becoming a chronic or hospitalized patient or to prevent escalation into impulsive and disturbed behaviour.

By keeping the security and care functions for those detained in TBS hospitals central, in the first place, adequate care is provided to those patients who need such care. Then, in daily practice, the patient as well as his assessors can find out whether he is prepared to allow treatment, because practice shows that a unit can be organized in such a way that the setting will motivate the patient to allow treatment. There are many implicitly motivating factors in the environment, like social learning (van Marle 1995). Treatment in a penitentiary institution means that the setting must offer such a psychological feeling of safety that the prisoner can rely on it, and dares to leave behind his own, often rigid, strategies. Moreover, there must be sufficient social learning situations in which he can experience all sorts of aspects and can exercise different behaviour. In the case of a total institution like a prison or a remand centre, this is not an easy task. A day programme must therefore be developed which is geared at the individual as much as possible, and in which this individual is offered as much freedom of choice and responsibility as possible (Smits 1994).

The chance to go from a security environment to an environment that provides care, and such by way of motivating the prisoner himself to allow treatment, is offered by the security environment itself. The security environment does not offer the chance for the prisoners to escape, so that they cannot run away from the problems they are confronted with within themselves. These security conditions themselves, however, may cause stress and aggression; in the case of nursing and care one should socialize in a specific way within this security restriction. If this mutual dependency and stereotyping of staff and prisoners, as Goffman (1961) explained, is not to remain permanent then this mutual dependency must be manipulated and developed towards a rather more differentiated socializing, more in line with the norm of society, with institutionally organized emphasis on respect for the individual and freely accessible treatment opportunities.

The penitentiary environment can then best be compared with the so-called holding environment (Winnicott 1979). Winnicott mentions the early mother–child relation and stresses that this relation is inseparable ('there is no such a thing as a baby'). One might claim, as Goffman did, that the relation between prisoners and warders or assessors in the security environment is also by definition inseparable. One is dependent on one other whether this is desired or not. As mentally disturbed prisoners are especially characterized by their immature, uncontrolled and impulsive behaviour, their behaviour requires a limit setting comparable to that necessary for young children. This holding environment, in which the prisoner is detained *and* cared for, can be built by fulfilling two basic conditions.

(1) Limit setting: both social conventions and legal aspects must be familiar to all concerned, staff as well as prisoners. The consequences regarding unacceptable behaviour will then be known and can be anticipated. Also for the staff a critical evaluation of their own behaviour must take place in cases where there is a danger of exceeding the limits. It is necessary at an early stage to prevent and keep in check threatening, aggressive behaviour. This influence has three levels, varying from directed at the patient himself to constructional circumstances in which the prisoner can be placed, like the degree of security of the unit or the padded-cell. On the other hand there must also be clear limits for staff. They too are part of the situation in which escalation of aggression takes place. These restrictions must also be found in the staff management and the terms of employment, in education and training, in the organizational structure of the penitentiary institution and decision-making.

(2) Diagnostics of transference relations: personnel and prisoners not only mutually influence each other on a conscious level but also on an unconscious level. The acting-out of disturbed prisoners is a familiar datum so that the organization is indeed geared to this. What is less known, however, is that in their work situation staff try to realize their own needs and wishes, which are not primarily linked to the targets of

this organization. This can anti-therapeutically influence the atmosphere in a certain unit. Developments in this direction must be detected and adjusted.

MOTIVATING FACTORS

The persons in question here will in the first place surely not be motivated from internal pressure of suffering to participate in a certain treatment. They are mostly characterized by the fact that they externalize the responsibility of their behaviour, i.e. blame others. A further problem in the treatment of these persons is also that for the greater part of their life they have not experienced any reliable emotional relations, because of the affective and pedagogical neglect in their youth. That is why compared with the average person they are less capable of entering into mutual relations and their attitude is particularly characterized by a distrust towards the other.

This combination of an absence of pressure of suffering, the incapacity to enter into a relationship, and a basic distrust of others, must be the first starting point for further interventions. It is true, these three factors are obstacles for a therapeutic treatment because in their presence no relationship with the therapist can develop. Motivating these persons and teaching them to look at themselves and to try to place themselves in somebody else's shoes, is the first task of the staff.

The unit setting must be adapted to this, so that the form of the detention situation and the essence of the approach are congruent with each other:

(1)   The prisoners must consistently be made aware of the consequences of their behaviour and how they can empathize with how the other feels as a result of their behaviour.

(2)   Procedures and decision-making must be clear and open, and fairness and the legal position must be central.

(3)   Staff must be present in the unit and approachable.

Something specifically is done with the mutual dependency, the 'spontaneous' reactions are detected in a special way and translated into interactions. With this attitude on the part of the staff, the experiences and emotions of those concerned will be detected and corrected.

Because of safety and tolerance this 'containment' consequently causes a motivating social environment. There is less stress among personnel and detainees, so there is less explosive aggression, which results in more opportunity for verbal exchange. To be forced to stay together results in reactions and interactions, and after that meaningful relations will develop in which earlier feelings and experiences will also play a role. The personnel facilitating verbal exchange can clarify both sides, and the recognition of the subjective reality of the person concerned (the 'empathy') will then develop the contact even further. To be continually dependent on each other with the experiences leading from this, will create 'social learning', in particular an unconscious process of copying efficient behaviour from each other. Finally, the clear cut separation between authority and dependence, linked to 'the total institution' (Goffman 1961), has substantial emotional similarities with the former family configuration so that unconscious repetition patterns will develop and can be interpreted.

PHASED ADAPTATION

The question now is how in such a secure setting we can promote a further psychological growth. This must in the first place start with the 'drive' with which the prisoner wishes to adjust his environment to one that suits him. He will try to include his direct environment in the acting out as a result of his personality problems. Naturally, these must be kept within certain, particularly safe, limits. The person in question will try to manipulate his environment so as to satisfy certain needs and values which confirm his partly conscious, partly unconscious self-image (enactment). The staff will interpret this enacting as an intrusion of the person in question to force them into a certain attitude towards him. So, this experience for the staff is an important diagnostic aid to see in which direction the patient develops from a psychological point of view. The staff must consequently be trained to detect and to give expression to these experiences.

The person in question can also be made conscious of this enactment by means of confrontation techniques so that he is not only confronted with his actual behaviour but is also taught, using psychotherapy or training programmes, how to find his way actively out of certain problems and how to provide alternative solutions. A precondition is that the living environment is not only limited because of the protection of society, which then offers a restriction of the possibilities to express oneself. Society's protection can, however, well be used as a precondition, by keeping the implementation of the security measures literally outside of the institution.

The security of the internal environment must be effected primarily on a relational basis by the attitude of the staff: preventive and de-escalating. Within this safeguarded environment there must also be possibilities for learning so that the prisoners can prepare themselves for the reintroduction to society. By making this environment as much as possible a reflection of normal society, all sorts of learning processes are encouraged. The persons in question are taught to socialize in a verbal not aggressive manner, so as to give them the experience that this way of acting can be advantageous for them, though not directly.

In between, on the one hand the field of the enactment on the basis of the personality disorders and on the other hand the environment of the institution as a social learning school, we find the task for the staff: to establish a link between the prisoner and the responsibility-improving environment. This link must be established consistently and can be considered a method. In fact the prison staff will have to familiarize themselves with all sorts of psychotherapeutic interventions, such as reflecting empathically, explaining and interpreting behaviour resulting from unexpressed motives. The profundity of the social attitude of the staff depends on the aim of the institution. In all instances it is advisable, though, to assign a supervisor to such a unit in the person of a (forensic) psychotherapist who monitors, interprets and sometimes clarifies the interaction between staff and prisoners.

The fact is that, in the interaction between staff and prisoners, for the latter group only demands should be put forward they can cope with. The limits of tolerance in the unit must therefore be flexible, but such that no physical aggression or any other unacceptable interpersonal behaviour will be tolerated. By keeping the treatment personally directed, so that each person concerned is required to do what he can cope with, one can avoid demanding too much from the prisoner. In this way a real self-confidence will develop.

It should not be forgotten that the environment structured in this way must in the end be internalized with the persons concerned. This means that the way of socializing, the level of pressure, and the dividing-line between what is just and what is unfair, should be transferred to the society in the final stages of the treatment. That is why a gradual resocialization is of paramount importance. As it happens, in the final stages the stress of therapeutic socializing can be decreased and the principles of social life can be introduced. It will in that case no longer be reasonable to continue the treatment of the persons in question using means similar to those for persons who have just entered the penitentiary environment. During the re-socialization phase much attention shall have to be paid to the fact that society will disappoint the prisoner and differs from the ideal image of the person in question and is different from his expectations regarding the future. The reactions to these disappointments will then have to be the primary focus of the interventions.

The result of this approach will be that the prisoners learn how to handle their ambivalence towards others, how to place themselves in somebody else's position and how to be able to postpone the fulfilment of their needs. The essence of this approach is to re-establish an attachment of the prisoner to his environment and from this to the persons living in this environment. From this attachment then, which must be encouraged actively, an internalization will occur inside the prisoner himself. However, this does not mean that this will be the case with everyone. This depends on the needs and the possibilities of each patient himself. But taking into consideration the primary dependency of the prisoner on the penitentiary environment, this attachment is centralized and encouraged from the start. Both prisoner and staff can do their utmost. The result will then be that they can detach themselves from each other again.

It is good to see that (partly influenced by the increased number of mentally disordered prisoners) an intricate system of support is being created within the prison system in the Netherlands in the form of various therapeutic or security units. This is mainly based on the selection of the various categories of disturbed and vulnerable prisoners. Although under the theory of criminal law, punishment and treatment are far removed from each other, in practice in the penal environment different opportunities for treatment appear to have been realized nonetheless.

2

Personality Disorders
The Paradigmatic Challenge to Psychotherapy

Murray Cox

'I have thee not, and yet I see thee still' (*Macbeth* II 1.35)

The thematic thread running throughout this paper is the crucial importance of establishing initial empathic contact with a personality disordered patient. This is the paradigmatic challenge. If this fails, therapy never starts and advanced stages of the therapeutic process are never reached.

There are many confluent concerns and Shakespearean promptings which have arisen in the discussion about personality disorders. Herman van Praag (1993) has emphasized the importance of accuracy and precision in scientific work and, from the outset, I shall refer to aesthetic accuracy, poetic precision and depth-activated aesthetic imagery. I hope to illustrate these phenomena in due course. I use the word aesthetic in Bateson's sense (1979) 'by aesthetic, I mean responsive to the pattern which connects' (p.17).

Some of the Shakespearean associations are as follows. She spoke 'as one incapable of her own distress' (*Hamlet* IV.7.177). This is what Gertrude said of Ophelia and it is of great psychotherapeutic significance. Psychotherapy is sometimes regarded as an activity which should remove or diminish distress, whereas it can be considered as a way in which individuals gradually become 'capable of their own distress'. This is closely linked to Pat Gallwey's comment about the therapist's task of staying with the patient during that unavoidable phase when things may be getting worse (1992).

We have heard of the importance of establishing trusting relationships, especially at the initial point of psychological contact. In Othello we hear these words: 'I pray you bring me on the way a little... 'Tis but a little way that I can bring you' (*Othello* III. 4, 196). The most we can ever do is to bring someone 'on the way a little'. Mention has been made of those occasions when we have to 'live on crumbs'. There is an ancient holding injunction which contains this key phrase 'gather up the fragments [the crumbs] that remain, that nothing may be lost' (*St John* 6, 12).

THE THING ITSELF

What is the essence? It is two-fold. One: Paradox. Though I have little to say that is new, except at the very end, the backbone of this presentation is the perennial importance of novelty. Two: the constraints of the compression of content, so that delivery is unrushed. I shall be speaking of *poiesis*, a crucial Greek word which means the 'calling into existence of that which was not there before' (Cox and Theilgaard 1987, p.23). It is of the essence of novelty – the unfamiliar. Assessing how the patient with a personality disorder deals with that with which he is unfamiliar is one of the important aspects of assessing therapeutic potential. This is why the aesthetic imperative is so useful, as I hope to demonstrate.

We are all indebted to Coid and Dolan (1993) for delineating treatment and research issues. At the beginning of their summary they say: '... that there is no evidence for the efficacy of a specific treatment. This should not be taken to mean that the treatment itself is ineffective, but rather that efficacy cannot be demonstrated from the available evidence' (p.261).

I speak as a jobbing forensic psychotherapist. My skills are in the exigencies of the present moment of therapeutic decision making... when to speak, when to keep silent, how to conduct the orchestra of the therapeutic group.

And now to paradigm.

PARADIGM

In what sense am I using the term? I'm returning to the words of Athanasius, by using the *paradeigma* as the theologian does.

> 'For this purpose [Athanasius] constructed and employed the concept of paradeigma which is not to be translated as "model" or "representation", far less as "archetype", but may be translated as "pointer", for it is essentially an operational term in which some image, idea or relation is taken... from experience to point beyond itself to what is quite new and so to help us get some kind of grasp upon it'. (Torrance 1969, p.16)

It is helpful to import the phrase of another theologian commentator, namely Melanchthon, who referred to: 'the courage to learn'.

When trying to establish contact with a patient with a personality disorder, we need 'to get some kind of a grasp'... 'I have thee not and yet I see thee still.' If we want a more left-brain title, we could borrow the title – though not a great deal of the content – of a paper by Myerson (1979) 'Issues of technique where patients relate with difficulty'.

One of the prime functions of time structuring in this chapter is to avoid that seductive, never-ending, potentially energy diverting preoccupation with technical terms, particularly when there is no single *fons et origo*. We have terms used by Freud, Klein, Kernberg, Kohut, Jung, Foulkes and all their neo-variants. Even so, that coined by Bollas (1987), namely extractive introjection is both inherently intriguing and has important forensic implications. 'Extractive introjection occurs when one person steals for a certain period of time (from a few seconds or minutes, to a lifetime) an element of another individual's psychic life' (p.158).

I have even been briefed prior to a formal lecture that 'we don't say archetypes here, we say deep structures'... or was it the other way round?

A recent experience has prompted a note of caution. Just before an interview on the BBC World Service about Shakespeare and The Mind, I was told 'Because of the global distribution of the audience (approximately 120,000,000) and therefore representing many different cultures, it would be preferable not to use technical terms'. This experience concentrated the mind wonderfully. Imagine trying to explain psychodynamic psychotherapy without reference to transference, countertransference, defence mechanisms, personality structure, externalization of a toxic introject, regression, idealization, not to forget extractive introjection and this huge cosmology of technical terminology!

Such a cosmos always carries the inherent risk that discussants play a kind of semantic academic verbal chess, in which one technical term is replaced by another, and there is the ever present danger that the human being will be ignored and located on an entirely different board.

For some reason or other, those important words of Falstaff's seem to be pressing at this point: 'Banish plump Jack, and banish all the world' (*I Henry IV*. II.4.473).

For this reason I shall use few technical terms and talk in images. Adopting this policy I'm in the good company of Masterson (1976). He referred to 'The six psychiatric horsemen of the apocalypse – depression, anger, fear, guilt, passivity and helplessness... [These] vie in their emotional sway and destructiveness with the social upheaval and destructiveness of the original four horsemen – famine, war, flood and pestilence. *Technical words are too abstract to convey the intensity and immediacy of these feelings and therefore the primacy they hold over the patient's entire life*' (p.38, emphasis added). I would also like to adopt the words of Davie (1964) when he said of the poet W.B. Yeats that he had: 'This way of standing by the image through thick and thin' (p.59).

I also take comfort from Foulkes (1990), whose descriptive simplicity is exemplary. Opening a paper at a congress in Vienna in 1968 he said: 'The best

I can do is to tell you how I work today... The group our patient now enters sits in a circle round a small table' (p.169).

Using an equally simple introduction, as our theme of talking in images develops, I quote from an early passage in *Mutative Metaphors* (Cox and Theilgaard 1987).

> I want to talk about something... but I want you to start it off because I don't know how. I can't start. I could use psychological jargon, like 'positive' or 'negative' feeling, but that is impersonal and uninvolved.'
>
> 'How about loving or hating?'
>
> 'That's nearer.'
>
> 'Or fire and ice?'
>
> 'That's it. That's me all over. There is no in between.' (The last phrase was said energetically immediately, and with a flash of relief and recognition on his face.) (p.8)

It is easy to see why loving and hating, and fire and ice, are the raw material of so much *poiesis* that leads to formal poetry. But poetry, in an orthodox sense, is not our concern here. Whereas the process of *poiesis*, in which 'something is called into existence which was not there before' is central and ubiquitous.

Two associations induced by the discussion of this theme refuse to remain silent:

> 'But from my grave across my brow
> Plays no wind of healing now,
> And fire and ice within me fight
> Beneath the suffocating night.'
> (Collected Poems, A.E. Housman, 1939)

> 'This is the Hour of Lead –
> Remembered, if outlived,
> As Freezing persons, recollect the Snow –
> First-Chill-then-Stupor – then the letting-go –' c. 1862
> (Complete Poems, Emily Dickinson 1970)

And here we are at paradox again. Listening has rightly been one of the main topics to which the trainee therapist's attention is addressed. I ask you to add up the number of seminars, lectures, papers and books – not to mention innumerable supervision sessions – when listening has been a central focus. But what about speaking?

And I am not referring to the formulation of the content of a psychoanalytic interpretation. For obvious reasons, every trainee will have considered this. On the contrary, I'm referring to the numerous other aspects of voice production, such as rhythm, cadence, intonational surge, differential enunciation, deictic stress and phatic language (Cox and Theilgaard 1994, p.225). Take a look at this sentence:

'*We are all only children.*'

Had we but world enough and time, I would ask you each to read this sentence and to discover how many possible meanings it conveys, depending upon differential emphasis. So it is in the enunciatory deixis within therapeutic space. It is simply not enough to record that a patient said: 'we are all only children'. Because, as it stands, its meaning is ambiguous.

AESTHETIC ACCESS TO THE PERSONALITY

When a new member had joined an established group and asked the others: 'What do you get out of the group?', she received a reply which surprised her: 'A pattern. A sequence. Something which stops me in my tracks and makes me stare.' Although the final comment had originally been referring to the impact of a work of art, it was adopted as having something important to say about group psychotherapy. This section of the presentation is condensed, but its content is of weight. A chain is no stronger than its weakest link. Similarly, effective affective bonding with a personality-disordered patient can depend on the existential immediacy of the initial contact. If this does not occur, however skilled the therapist and however ultimately motivated the patient, there may be no chance for the developmental line within therapeutic space to take root. The initial stages are crucial.

One of the most daunting prospects of my life was when I was about to set off on a mountain walk in Norway. There were sheer walls of rockface, with a perfectly adequate path cut originally by nature, and assisted by man, so that hundreds of feet of vertical wall arose above and fell away below the path.

To someone such as myself, who is phobic about heights even in Holland, it was psychic trauma of an acute form to be told that it would be a beautiful and challenging walk, apart from the first 25 meters where the path had fallen away! The analogy speaks for itself. Initial contact and the possibility of movement in the right direction, however faltering, are vital both within the paradigmatic therapeutic challenge posed by the personality-disordered patient, and when setting out along a mountain path.

Inadequate initial bonding within a secure relationship on a potentially threatening route is vital.

Previous presentations have referred to the importance of early intervention and remind us of key publications on the ethos of assessment interviews and initial therapeutic sessions (Bruch 1974; Argelander 1976).

MUTATIVE METAPHORS AND INITIAL THERAPEUTIC PHASES

One day I entered a group therapy room in Broadmoor and found the air full of cushions, which were being thrown from one patient to another, for all the world resembling bulky padded 'frisbees'. Had I adopted a patronizing authoritarian air and suggested that we should now get down to the serious business of group psychotherapy and give up these childish games, I am certain (at least I hope) that I would have been ignored and that the playful creativity would continue. On the other hand, when I took my seat and suggested that we were all like the frisbees, being thrown into life, into families and maybe into prison or adjacent seats in a therapeutic group, the participants immediately sat and took the theme with interest. Although I did not refer to Heidegger or Buber, their thoughts were certainly in my mind as we explored various facets of man's state of thrownness into his existential predicament. This I suggest, was a creative use of chaos. It illustrated aesthetic access to the life of the group through the use of the mutative metaphor. Once again, it emphasizes the importance of novelty and the creative use of chaotic playfulness, which so often lends its stamp to the opening of the therapeutic session.

THE INITIAL MEETING WITH A NEW PATIENT

The last patient I saw for an assessment interview prior to leaving for this conference had this to say: 'My father poured boiling water over me to try to wash the colour out of my skin. My mother threw me... on to an open fire. I hate anyone who tries to get near me'.

He found difficulty in trusting. Why should he trust anyone after this fearful experience? Particularly other 'parental' figures who approached him hoping to be trusted. There was virtually nothing on which to obtain any affective purchase. Continuing the climbing analogy, there was virtually nothing on which to obtain a handhold. Is initial empathy with such a patient possible?... 'I have thee not, and yet I see thee still.' Here paradox can be at its most profound. Bachelard writes: 'But the image has touched the depths before it stirs the surface' (Bachelard 1969, p.xix, see Cox and Theilgaard 1987, p.xiii).

The patient sullenly rehearsed the advantages and disadvantages of a prison sentence versus an unlimited time in Broadmoor, 'But here is a long time'.

At this juncture I need to look at things in a little more detail, because aesthetic access to the personality can suggest an adequate psychological 'handhold' if conceptual distortion is linked to unusual enunciatory emphasis. In this instance, the patient had confused the usual distinction between Now and Then, Here and There. He spoke of Here in relation to Time, rather than Place. The inductive effect of Shakespearean prompting at this precise point was that embedded in his sentence 'here is a long time', I 'heard' (as though it was in the margin). 'But in these cases we still have *judgement here*.' This is an association from *Macbeth* (I.7.7) and this led me to ask the patient: 'What is your *judgement* on yourself?'.

This was the aesthetic imperative at work. This tiniest handhold did indeed suggest affective purchase. Returning to the phrase about the art gallery: 'it stopped him in his tracks and made him stare'. (It is impossible to amplify this important dynamic process further here. But an emotional bridge-head was established in that moment. It is virtually the central theme of *Shakespeare as Prompter: The Amending Imagination and The Therapeutic Process*, Cox and Theilgaard 1994).

In summary, we note that patients with personality disorders, who normally prefer to divide stimuli into those which are ego-alien and those which are ego-syntonic, feel 'unsettled' with those novel stimuli to which they cannot habituate. The novelty inherent in creativity implies that the patient cannot safely categorize that which is new. For this reason he is unable to marshall his conscious defensive strategies and is more accessible to 'benign' confrontation with himself in the presence of the therapist. In this way substantial initial bonding can occur, so that the patient is actually keen on the second session when he can take this exploration further. I can recall several occasions when a patient with a reputation of never seeing an 'assessor' on more than one occasion, would tell me 'Actually I have written poetry myself. I will bring it next time you come.' This being long before I had even raised the possibility of a second session!

DEPTH-ACTIVATED AESTHETIC IMAGING

This is the name given to a heightened form of focal *aesthetic access*, in which the depths of a personality are assessed without stirring the surface (Cox and Theilgaard 1994, p.364). It has the paradoxical quality of a benign depth-charge. It is 'disturbing', because its inherent novelty resists habituation. It should be noticed that depth-activated aesthetic imaging can be verbal or visual. Indeed it can be poly-sensory. But in this chapter my illustrative examples have been verbal. I have previously published a vignette (Cox 1983, p.98) in which a patient who had hitherto refused to speak about his index offence, found himself unable to refrain from describing the incident in explicit detail, following an indirect, allusive reflective question, '...I wonder why death's flag is so pale'? (I will not give detail here, but refer the reader to the original publication).

Here is a final example of the extreme simplicity of metaphorical translocation. A teasing provocatively manipulative patient put a vase of flowers on the corner of a desk in the direct line of sight between her eyes and mine. This gesture was meant to ridicule such therapeutic progress as there was and to divert attention. I responded in an unexpected way. 'Sally, this is a moment I have been waiting for… This is the first time that "Honesty" has come between us!' After that enigmatic confrontation, therapy proceeded apace! (The flower in question is known as Honesty in English. For obvious reasons, the example had an entirely different effect in Denmark, where I discovered that the same flower carries the name Judas Money!).

In *The Political Psyche*, Samuels (1993, p.70) refers to two styles of 'patholo-gizing' which he describes as the 'professional' and the 'poetic'. Having referred to the fact that these two polarities are not in opposition, he takes us close to the aesthetic imperative (Cox and Theilgaard 1987, p.26) in this memorable phrase 'the professional cutting edge of an acute poetic imagination'. This is intrinsically linked to the transformative power, inherent in the mutative metaphor, which can sometimes mobilize autogenous interpretations. These are usually more efficacious and have greater chance of attaining emotional purchase, because they arise within the patient himself.

Clinical Vignette

A female patient of 37 is reliving a childhood experience. In a therapeutic group she describes how, as a girl of five or six, she was wading into a fast flowing stream wearing her Wellington boots. As she got deeper into the stream it was both exciting and frightening. She could feel the water level rising higher and higher, until it flowed over the top of her boots, and gave her a tingling feeling in her legs as the water level rose. At the moment when the stimulus became almost unbearable, she suddenly saw two large eels swimming towards her. They were menacing, and she could not be sure which direction they would take and was therefore unable to avoid them. Furthermore, she could not run fast because her boots were full of water. Her anxiety was evident in the group. Breathless and sweating, she suddenly turned to me and said 'Is that why I am afraid of penises?'

An autogenous realization of this nature has a self-authenticating im-perative, which is often far more powerful, than a technical 'interpretation' from a therapist.

UP-DATING FREUD'S MILITARY METAPHOR

A constant theme of theoretical speculation relates to the way in which the history of psychoanalysis might have taken a different course, if Freud had chosen some other metaphorical system than that of the military language of attack and defence, invasion and retreat. Had he, for example, used musical analogies, we should be speaking in terms of harmony, discord, resolution, modulation, development, recapitulation, transposition, rhythm, pitch and cadence. In fact the therapeutic energies of mutative metaphors would have been equally beneficial. Thus a 'pivot chord' which is common to two keys, would be a useful source of therapeutic and supervisory energy.

Nevertheless, there is a fascinating new range of metaphors which make the original military metaphor so much more dynamic. I refer to the modern generation of munitions, which are drawn towards a target which has previously been pin-pointed with laser precision. We are told that it emits a laser spectrum known as a 'basket'. The heat-seeking sensor on the munition approaches the laser basket so that it cannot fail to reach the target. Space, time and my exceedingly restricted knowledge of the subject prevent further development, except to point out that the munition is guided on its trajectory by the fact that it is object-seeking and heat-seeking.

Thus, it is directly analogous to object-relations theory. If, for a moment, we think of the history of bombing strategies, originally, the bomb aimer lent over the side of the plane and tried to literally drop the bomb on the target. The next generation of bomb aimers was far more scientific, depending on the calculation of the final common path, taking account of velocity, height, prevailing winds and the like. It seems to me that an entirely different range of forces is now taken into consideration whereby the target, as it were, draws the bomb upon itself.

Even so, as we are concerned with nourishing energies, growth and therapy, I would prefer to use metaphors culled from modern military technology which might be linked to laser-guided 'drops' of food and medical equipment, rather than agents of destruction. There is surely an elaborate metaphor awaiting elucidation here. The example just cited about the girl in her Wellington boots who was 'afraid of penises' is a case in point. In other words, she draws the threatening symbolic object towards herself, but the psycho-sexual significance is rendered tolerable, because it occurs at a depth and pace for which she is prepared. Such depth-activated aesthetic imaging has already been described as having some of the qualities of a benign depth-charge (Cox and Theilgaard 1994, p.364). Our final words come from Foulkes (1964). 'It would be of the utmost interest to study deviant groups such as delinquents, criminals or psychopaths in general in pure culture and see whether they, as a group or individually, do really essentially deviate from others or not' (p.298).

We are fortunate indeed to find ourselves working in a field of such 'utmost interest' in which personality disorders provide the paradigmatic challenge and we end by returning to the first sentence which referred to the importance of establishing initial empathic contact. This paper has explored some avenues of access which can help to bring this about.

3

Forensic Psychotherapy and the Empirical Paradigm

Friedemann Pfäfflin

Looking at the situation of psychotherapy and psychoanalysis in Germany we have been trusting credos for all too long. High frequency psychoanalysis, interpretation of transference and understanding countertransference, we believed, would be the best forms of treatment. Now, in times of economical recession and increasing public poverty, and with the upswing of alternative psychotherapies, this belief is heavily challenged. Coverage of psychoanalytic treatment is being restricted in respect to frequency of sessions per week as well as the sum total of treatment sessions. In a number of important and widely quoted studies (see for an overview Grawe, Donati and Bernauer 1994) the efficacy of psychoanalytic treatment is questioned as compared with the efficacy of cognitive and behavioural treatments. Instead of beliefs, customers and health-care providers ask for proofs. Psychotherapy outcome research and psychotherapy process research are becoming more and more important.

Beyond beliefs, in a scientific organization such as the International Association for Forensic Psychotherapy, we will have to check if it is really true that using metaphors as a psychotherapeutic agent will promote fundamental change, and we will have to demonstrate it to those who are in charge of public safety. 'But the image has touched the depths, before it stirs the surface' – Murray Cox's favourite quotation of Gaston Bachelard (Cox and Theilgaard 1987, p.xiii) – is a wonderful image but, of course, being involved in the treatment of serious criminals, we also want to be sure that it will eventually stir the surface, resulting in observable changes of criminal behaviour.

Some fifteen years ago I had a severely disturbed patient with obsessive-compulsive fantasies about killing his male lovers (Pfäfflin 1981, 1992). This patient, at the same time, had a great ability to find and use metaphors himself.

During my holiday, for example, he wrote me letters, or rather a diary, which he called 'the bridge across twelve hours' – one page for every therapy session missed. Thus, he was able to fill the gap in our continuous dialogue caused by my absence. This was just one of his many and very impressive metaphors. Some years later, having committed a comparatively minor attempt to attack one of his partners, when he had been admitted by the court to a psychiatric hospital some hundred miles away, so that we could not continue treatment, he managed to escape from that institution and actually put his terrible fantasies into practice. His metaphors were not strong enough to keep him from falling into a deep gorge.

Clinical convictions are important; consensus of groups of experts as to what works, what promotes change, is of paramount interest. Therapeutic success relies heavily on a trustable patient–therapist relationship, but one wants to know what the components of such a working alliance are; another one is that metaphors may create the experience of novelty and thus promote change. Yet, to demonstrate that such convictions are not the circular results of beliefs, we will have to study psychotherapeutic processes in a replicable manner and in such ways that the result of such research can be taught and promoted to future psychotherapists.

There are now a number of researchers and institutions that have developed detailed methodologies for evaluating psycho-therapeutic processes. Most of the researchers involved are members of the Society for Psychotherapy Research (SPR). It would take more than one chapter to discuss the methods and results of their work. Only a few, therefore, very briefly, may be mentioned. It was D.P. Spence (1968, 1970) who initiated the computerized evaluation of psychotherapy sessions. Hartvig Dahl (1972, 1974, 1979), at the Downstate Medical Centre, New York State University, developed a guide for the standardized and uniform transcription of psychotherapy sessions, which became widely used by researchers and thus laid the foundation for comparisons of the results of the computerized evaluation of therapy sessions. These standards have been improved by Mergenthaler and Stinson (1992).

In 1979 Kächele and Mergenthaler from the Department of Psychotherapy of Ulm University, Germany, started to pursue the plan of a centralized archive of psychotherapy data sources, which, through the support of the German Research Foundation was finally achieved in 1980. The Ulm Text Bank (UTB) meanwhile has become the world's largest collection of reports, test protocols, tapes and transcripts, open for scientists from all over the world, but, of course, with strict rules as regards confidentially of data (Mergenthaler and Kächele 1991). In a second paper these authors (Mergenthaler and Kächele 1993) described the Ulm Text Bank and compared its resources and regulations with two other archives devoted to psychotherapy process research (Psychoanalytic Research Consortium (PRC), founded in 1989 by Sherwood Waldron, New York, and the Centre for the Study of Neuroses (Director Mardi Horowitz), State University of California, San Francisco). What seems important here is that not one of them has ever studied therapy in a forensic setting.

I would like to invite everybody who is working as a psychotherapist in the forensic field to cooperate in the evaluation of the therapeutic processes for this special group of patients. We then may find out if these patients are really almost inaccessible, as is often said, or if we just declare them to be so different from other patients, to explain away the shortcomings of our therapeutic skills. Kingsley Norton says in his chapter, to quote just one of the contributors to this conference, that 'these people do not use words as you and I do'. I doubt that. Perhaps we also use words differently because we know they are criminals; or perhaps we should use them differently to make ourselves better understood and to find a proper access.

One of the most widespread ways of teaching psychotherapy is through supervision. Empirical evaluation of therapy transcripts is a second route, another paradigm, which may be communicated and taught to much larger audiences. This allows us to verify or falsify the importance of metaphors, and may lead us to detect additional important factors in the therapeutic process of which we do not even know yet. For most psychotherapists the language of empirical research seems dead and dull, with all its numbers, statistics and correlations. I must admit, before I moved to Ulm one and a half years ago, and started to cooperate with the Ulm Text Bank, I shared the same bias.

When trained in a traditional psychoanalytic way, it does take some time to get acquainted with the language of empirical psychotherapy process research, to detect its advantages, and finally, to distinguish its poetry and melody which, no doubt, are as apt as metaphors to animate and invigorate the psychotherapeutic potential we need to meet the needs of our special patients.

PART TWO

Treatment Issues

4

To Treat or Not To Treat
The Therapeutic Challenge

Estela Welldon

CHALLENGING EXPERIENCES

I am first and foremost a clinician and as such I believe that the only way to make any working theoretical hypothesis about how the mind works is through clinical observations. I do not agree with a colleague's remark: 'never listen to your patients, because if you do, they will ruin all your theories!'.

After becoming a teacher, specializing in children with Down Syndrome, I decided to go to medical school in order to further my studies in that area and become a child psychiatrist. During medical school I entered into psychoanalysis where I was able to work through some of my own rebelliousness and anti-authority feelings. This may have had an influence in the shift of my interest from learning disabilities to delinquency and crime. I believe my psychoanalyst then was rather pleased with this new development since at the time it was thought it would involve a more hopeful outcome.

I had a very short professional career in my home town, since a few months after I qualified, I was expected to start my post-graduate studies at the Menninger School of Psychiatry in the USA. Still, it left me enough time to work in a local Borstal for girls. There I had my first, but unforgettable, contact with the dangers attached to working in a dictatorial, hierarchical and auto-cratic setting, a setting which consciously or unconsciously existed for the benefit of the staff authorities and hence resulted in the detriment of those deprived, rebellious children who were supposed to be taken care of. My work there lasted exactly three days. My first day started with my seeing a girl of thirteen with long dark hair being rude and loud to a staff member, having being provoked by the latter. The girl was taken away and a few minutes later

31

was brought back with her head shaven. She seemed shaken, but was not showing any of it.

I was furious with the authorities, but not speechless. I made it clear that my resignation would be automatically offered if a similar situation ever happened again. This did not take long. My resignation was handed in three days later, when another girl was subjected to the same fate.

Amongst other things that I learnt effectively from this was how *not* to work in an arrogant and lonesome position without regard for the team.

On my arrival at the Menningers, I was placed as a psychiatrist in charge of a maximum security ward treating dangerous patients. I had begun to settle down nicely, having achieved some degree of familiarity with the patients, when suddenly we were confronted with most sensational news in the local paper. The cover page showed a picture of a young Asian woman, three small children, the open door of an icebox full of food and the headlines: *Mother killed children by means of starvation.* The following day, a 27-year-old woman from Okinawa, married to a black American soldier, was charged with the killing of her three children and brought to our ward. When I first got to know of her impending admission, I was filled with preoccupations of how this new patient would be received by the others. I was worried about the possibility of other violent patients attacking her, on account of the killings of her own small children.

There is always a lot to learn from an anticipated response, especially when it proves to be wrong. It makes you very humble and rethink it all over again. All in all, not a bad thing.

As soon as the young woman, who was in complete distress, came into the ward, all the patients greeted her with the warmest and yet most adequate welcome. I still remember a male patient with both arms amputated being particularly nice to her. He had himself cut his arms off with a guillotine in his own butcher's shop after killing both his wife and her lover. Our new patient did constitute a real challenge for treatment, but it would take a long time to tell about it. Suffice it to say that I believe she brought with her a challenge to the most disturbed fellow patients in the ward. She may unwittingly have been the best milieu therapist in the ward.

My next post was at the Kansas Diagnostic and Reception Center, a maximum security unit for criminals where I worked for a few months before leaving for the UK. Here, on asking the prison officers to bring to me an inmate for a psychodynamic psychiatric evaluation, they would promptly do so by bringing to me the man with arms and legs in chains. I found this not to be the most facilitating setting for any patient to develop a sense of trust in his psychiatrist!

Later, on my arrival to the UK, I was most fortunate in finding a training post at the Henderson Hospital. This unit had been founded by Maxwell Jones with the aim of the treatment of psychopathic personalities – today, so-called personality disorders. The Henderson gave me a renewed sense of trust as a therapeutic place which existed for the benefit of the patients and not of the staff. The enormous challenge of their treatment was met by a sound and adequate structure of democracy and division of labour in which everyone, patients and staff, shared not only the burden of their treatment, but also the administration of the hospital.

Admission and discharge procedures were only a part of the philosophy of the place in which patients had their say, regrettably so at times for me. I remember often getting back to London in tears in the train feeling so angry and frustrated with the 'bloody community' for discharging a patient who had broken the existing rules and who I thought I could have successfully treated if they had only been allowed to stay. It took me a long time to learn that the community knew better than myself. It was the arrogance of the medical profession which made me feel otherwise.

At the time of my starting work there, the medical director, an elderly gentleman, was away on leave. Two weeks later, the nice 'honeymoon' established between the community and myself was suddenly and unexpectedly brought to a close. On his return, the medical director announced in the community meeting his decision to retire in a month's time. This took everyone by surprise, which was later replaced by the patients' indignation and tremendous grief. Fantasies ran very far and gave me a strong sense of the powerful transferential response evoked in these patients when faced with separation from someone they have learnt to trust.

Delinquent behaviour was rife. Shoplifting excursions to the local shops, joyriding and pregnancies were few ways of expressing their distress. Patients were devastated and disappointed about the old man's departure and angry, even livid at my own staying. The split was very effective since they saw him as a frail and fragile nice old man and me as the rotten young bitch ready to take him over.

Common sense did not succeed in any interpretation. On the contrary, for many days to come, at the time of the doctors' group (a therapeutic group run as a small group by each doctor), patients of my small group formed a circle around me, spitting all sorts of verbal abuse with the occasional attempt to throw a chair at me. The fact that the chair never hit me gave me the hint they did not really want to get rid of me. This was quite an improvement since it indicated a change from the physical to the verbal expression of powerful feelings. Still, this powerful negative transference was not easy to take, even if intellectually understood. That was a therapeutic challenge that had to be taken seriously. I then learnt of the powerful countertransferential response evoked in myself, which made me feel vengeful, angry and sad.

As usual, with the help of my colleagues, I was able to understand more and more about our patients' early emotional deprivations and their ways of dealing with 'acting out' behaviour. That was their way of expressing their bereavement for someone they had valued and missed and their hate for me for staying with them. Despite my initial reaction of wanting to leave immediately, this being my own acting out, I decided to stay. The following three years gave me a wonderful share of the community life with the richest interaction between patients and staff. Days were full with new learning which included at times much pain, but also unexpected reward observing those patients, who were able to leave the Community after achieving inner changes. I experienced this too; life outside had become unreal, seemingly pale, lifeless and stale, in comparison with my working time, expecting the Henderson's full vitality to be forever present.

My next post took me to the Paddington Day Hospital in London, where the experience from the therapeutic community was to be used in similar ways. The new challenge was how to cope effectively with massive acting out on Friday afternoons, when the community had to depart for the weekend. Once more staff and patients had a different perspective. Weekends were eagerly waited by staff members for a well deserved rest, and dreaded by patients, who were ready to commit suicide at the prospect of being on their own.

TRANSFERENCE AND COUNTERTRANSFERENCE

A different challenge altogether was offered when I started working at the Portman Clinic twenty-three years ago. This was by comparison the most formal place with an extremely well defined hierarchical system. It is a NHS out-patient clinic which offers individual psychoanalytical psychotherapy to patients who suffer from perversions and/or who engage in acts of delinquency and crime. Angry confrontations were the exception, not the rule, with the occasional acting out behaviour from the patients. To start with, this took me by surprise. Were psychoanalytical interpretations more effective, or were patients different, less disturbed?

It took me some time to realize that patients who share some personality characteristics are, at different times of their lives, more or less susceptible to treatment in different settings. So, not only has treatability to be assessed, but the choice of the forensic setting is of essential importance. There are those who need much containment, safety and nourishment when younger or more disturbed. However, these therapeutic elements should be provided for a limit of one year, otherwise institutionalization could easily set in, jeopardizing any meaningful inner changes. The split is then established: we, the insiders are the good, the outside is the dreadful and hostile world.

At the Portman I began to learn of the subtleties involving transferential and countertransferential processes which include the patients' need for control, their apparently jocular attitude, which effectively covers distress and isolation; their attempts to seduce the therapist in collusion and unconscious participation with their delinquent behaviour.

I shall always be grateful to our senior colleagues, the 'oldies and goldies' who enabled their juniors to deal competently with those difficult predicaments. However, occasionally I was also glad to have evidence of their being able to make mistakes too! Shortly after my arrival at the Portman, and anxious to have as many difficult patients as possible, I was allocated to a young, attractive, recently married man with a bizarre sexual perversion. This, he told me, involved the use of very complicated rubber gear all over his body, including head and limbs, with the aim of producing an almost total sensory deprivation, at which point he would reach orgasm. If anything went wrong he would face death.

I met this therapeutic challenge with some fear and with wanting to know more. I was painfully aware that my knowledge of the subject was scarce and inadequate. In my search for more information, I was quite careless and decided on a Saturday morning while doing my weekly grocery shopping in Soho, to enter a so called 'sex shop' where I could learn more about the quality of the desired rubber. To my bewilderment I found out that the rubber, till then assumed by me to be of the kind used for underwater sports, was actually quite different. It was as thin as a second skin, to be used over the body. This new knowledge gave me immediate access to meanings and symbolisms to which I had been previously blind.

But there were other unsuspected problems to be faced that Friday morning when presenting my patient in the clinical seminar to the rest of the staff. In doing so, I explained my sense of inadequacy and my excursion to the sex shop. This was not kindly taken. Indeed, the opposite. Suddenly my seniors were up in arms, alarmed at my alleged collusion and partnership with my patient's perversion. I felt humiliated and misunderstood. All interpretations were made at my countertransference reaction in my being seduced by my patient. I found this very difficult to take. I got a sudden inspiration and presented a challenge back to them. If any of them knew the exact nature of the rubber employed for this man's perversion, I would accept without hesitation their interpretations of my own 'acting out'. However, if nobody could offer an adequate description of the rubber, their 'judgement' of the situation had to be reviewed, since my 'detour' would be considered of a scientific nature and not an acting out. This was eventually accepted with some reluctance. To my relief and delight a description of the thick rubber used for underwater protection was offered.

I was now able to explain what the rubber was really like and we all were able to participate in a rich exchange of ideas. Anyway, it was a narrow escape. So much for the rough learning of the implications of transference and countertransference in working with the forensic patient.

GROUP PSYCHOTHERAPY

I began to think that psychoanalytical group therapy could also present a worthwhile challenge, considering its potential benefits for such 'antisocial' and 'asocial' people. In the early days the Portman staff almost gave up hope, because so many patients did not return after their first session. We were forced then to think again about our whole approach. Once more, modification of the classical techniques were needed. I would like to record and emphasize here how rewarding our experience in implementing a program of working with group techniques has been. These patients offer a great challenge, which they cherish when offered an opportunity for therapy and it is gratifying to see how much they can change. In my view when working with personality disordered patients, the therapeutic task is to facilitate a movement towards acting less and suffering more, whereas with neurotics, it is to help them to suffer less and to act more.

In my own case, the experience of working at the Henderson Hospital was invaluable. Painfully, but effectively, we learnt how to allow active confrontation when we felt the patients needed firm leadership to relieve their own anxieties about ineffectual, uncaring parental figures. This was a far cry from former rigorous training, in which the instrument of therapy and learning was limited to interpretation of the here and now dynamics and to the group as a whole.

Colleagues are often reluctant to take these patients for group therapy. They refer to the 'facts', meaning that these patients either do not respond to this type of therapy, or that it may be effective only if one such patient is integrated into a 'neurotic' group. These 'facts' are myths, however: they do not derive from experience. Moreover, these myths contain prejudices which could easily produce some serious consequences.

First, these patients are left without the benefit of being able to interact with the social microcosm which occurs in group therapy and which could afford them a much better understanding of their problems since they are so deeply related to antisocial actions. Second, these prejudices professionally isolate the therapist who works with this type of patient, since critics assume that these patients cannot be treated in a group setting. Consequently, there are very few colleagues with whom to share the richness of material emerging from working with 'antisocial' patients who have problems related to violence.

I was at first inclined to explain these myths by relating them to unconscious mechanisms arising from the critics' enormous fear of the inner emergence of the same mental mechanisms in themselves. This would result in the splitting off from society, not only of this type of patient, but also of their therapists, both through fear and as a means of punishment. However, further thought suggests a different view which has to do not only with all the intricacies in changes of technique already noted, but also with the formal setting in which these patients are treated. Experience at the Portman Clinic has made it increasingly clear in the last few years how much our patients' psychopathologies are intertwined in the transference process not only with their peer group, but also with the institution treating them. This can become as, or more important than the therapist himself. The formal setting is essential for their treatment. Even the physical location counts, as we at the Portman Clinic well know. We very much value our large Victorian house since it provides us all with a warm and homely atmosphere.

When I began to develop a group analytical programme I became more aware of the enormous disparity in the ratio of men patients compared to women – another split emerged: men are perverted and women are neurotic (Welldon 1996).

Since men had appealed to perversion as a way to deal with the fears of losing their penis, women were left in a position in which perversions were not available to them. As women do not have a penis, so the argument went, they must have a different type of Oedipus complex and castration anxiety. Hence then the popular view that 'Women can't have sexual perversions since they don't possess a penis' was seldom questioned. Freud theorized that the Oedipus complex was resolved in little girls when they fantasized having Daddy's babies inside themselves. Developing his ideas, we could say provocatively that 'Women can't have perversions because they can have babies' (Welldon 1992). This was the background which led to the development of my book (1988) which is the first attempt to study female sexual perversions. For this I drew only on my own clinical experience, but was also grateful for discussion with other members of the Portman staff about their own experience.

ASSESSMENT

In order to assess treatability for psychotherapy accurately in these patients, we must modify terms and concepts from those used in assessing neurotic patients. For example, when the criminal action is committed clumsily, the person is especially susceptible to detection. The criminal action has become the equivalent of the neurotic symptom. The offender may also express fears of a custodial sentence, which may denote, in his own terms, motivation for treatment. This could signal that it is the appropriate time to start treatment, since the patient is susceptible; however, much under implied duress. He is now ready to own up to his psychopathology and this may denote an incipient sense of capacity for insight.

From this therapeutic standpoint, it is not unfortunate that a patient has to face prosecution, but what is unfortunate is that just when he is ready for treatment, he may instead have to face punishment. The patient may actually acquire a criminal record for the first time while in treatment or on the waiting list. Ironically, the very success of our treatment may produce this result. It is when the patient, who has hitherto escaped detention, starts to acquire some insight into himself that he becomes clumsy and is detected. So, in a way, it may be said that psychotherapy results in a higher rate of official, statistical criminality!

In the selection criteria for psychotherapy it is vital first to make a basic distinction between offenders who are mentally disordered and those who are not. Some offenders have a professional orientation towards their criminal activities. For example, they calculate the consequences, even going so far as to engage in a cost-benefit planning of their actions, involving such matters as how many months or years in prison they are prepared to risk. In other words, such offenders may not differ in important psychological traits from careerists generally. These two seemingly different categories do at times overlap or succeed one another. It is not unusual to find patients who have been criminal 'careerists' for a number of years, but who on reaching their thirties begin to question the validity of what they are doing and express a deep interest in seeking professional help to change their life-styles.

A woman in her thirties was referred by the Court on account of shoplifting. The first time I saw her she seemed duly upset about the nature of the offence. She had been caught in Woolworths steeling sheets and underwear worth £28.40. It later transpired that the reason she felt terrible was the fact that the theft was so petty and insignificant. This took place after eight years of impeccable behaviour, and after her only child, a boy, was born. This present offence was very uncharacteristic of her earlier, flamboyant offending behaviour and it caused her great shame and embarrassment. After all these years during which she had resisted all temptation what had caused her to relapse in the way that she had? She had resorted to crime again, but this time she had acted in such a clumsy way, something that she had always promised herself never to do.

Initially I took the statement at its face value. On second thoughts, though, I considered that the offence had been meticulously, but unconsciously de-signed. Had she relapsed into her usual style, she would have been automat-ically sent to prison without the advantage of seeking professional help. Instead, by committing the offence in such a clumsy and virtually profitless way, she seemed to be expressing a new move, a change in her inner life (from careerist to symptom). This woman at the age of 33 perhaps felt that the time was ripe for her to find help and make the most of it. In other words, she was ready to give up the false self and to explore who she really was. She was experiencing an incipient awareness of a sense of futility. She began to see herself as a pathetic and hopeless middle-aged woman, instead of the glamorous little princess she had been brought up to believe she was.

At other times the criminal action may indicate another important characteristic, that is, the manic defence, created against the acknowledgement or recognition of a masked chronic depression.

At other times the offence may include compulsion, impulsiveness, inability to intersperse thought before action and a total failure to understand it.

A patient of 38 wrote to me regarding his exhibitionistic behaviour:

> It has been ever present from age thirteen and has now become a matter of urgent concern. Although throughout my life I have been able to conceal this from everyone including my wife and my close associates at work, I am now taking many risks. I am scared of being caught any minute. Previously I had been careful and cunning in my flashing, going to places far away from home and work. But now I am experiencing the need to do it in nearby places, or in a repetitive fashion either to the same women or in the same places or at the same times. I have found that this taking risks has become now my only way to be able to relieve myself from increasing sexual anxiety. I am unable to bear this any longer.

This dynamic, changing characteristic contains a positive element. It is basic to acknowledge this since it enables us to make more accurate diagnosis and better treatment recommendations.

At times this process takes place during the course of psychotherapy and it denotes an improvement of the condition, though this is not easily acknowledged.

RELATIONSHIP WITH THE THERAPIST

Separation anxieties can easily produce most dangerous acting out. Gallwey (1991) remarks on this sort of occurrence that 'The uncovering of areas of deprivation and unfulfilled dependency can produce enormous pressure on both therapist and patient, with a speedy move into delinquent acting out, or even violence, when the patient feels let down or abandoned within the therapy. The least hazardous tactic is to contain the individual in a way which minimises the reinforcement of delinquent strategies' (p.368). Therapists' holidays are very distressing for patients in treatment since they feel neglected, abandoned and uncared for, just as they did when they were infants. There are often, however, signals in the sessions leading up to holidays that 'something is going on'. It is important to detect and recognize these clues, for they form part of this constellation or syndrome responsible for 'acting out' behaviour. It may be seen as a resistance to the therapeutic process (Welldon 1984).

The relapse in delinquent and criminal behaviour is frequently found during the first long holiday in psychotherapy. This is associated with feelings of having been abandoned by the therapist at a time of need.

The importance of money in both concrete and symbolic terms is obvious with patients whose day-to-day living is provided by their own or close associates' delinquent or perverse actions. As in the previous example, a frequent problem is the offer or 'pushing' of a gift which could at times render the therapist a receiver of stolen goods. This is another powerful reason for treatment of the forensic patient to be provided by the State. The therapists' inner knowledge that the State is paying for their professional services, becomes invaluable while working with this patient population, since they are also aware of this basic fact. It reinforces both parties in the contractual agreement on which the therapy is based. The therapists are debarred from blackmail and the patients feel neither exploited nor able to exploit anybody about money matters.

In the course of treatment, a female patient of 27 charged with soliciting, started to develop a 'sense of trust' towards me. This was in open contrast with the initial phase when she had been very reluctant to engage in treatment, and had mocked the hypocritical moral middle class standards. Her husband was a notorious bank robber who had managed never to be detected. In the sessions she told me of her anxieties regarding his activities.

One day, she surprised me by saying: 'Doctor, I trust you so much that you are going to be the only person to know of my husband's next job. But if the information leaks to the police, I will know that you are not trustworthy'. With this provocative statement she was challenging me with undisclosed information about her husband's impending 'job'. As opposed to indicating a 'sense of trust' she was placing me in a double bind position. I could easily feel threatened and ready to be blackmailed, or I could become a partner in crime.

PERSONALITY DISORDERS

The forensic patient is unable to think before the action occurs, because he is not mentally equipped to make the necessary links (Bion 1959). His thinking process is not functioning in his particular area of perversity which is often encapsulated from the rest of his personality. Therefore this is the work of therapy, but at times the patient's tendency to make sadistic attacks on his own capacity for thought and reflection is projected and directed against the therapist's capacity to think and reflect, and it is then that the therapist feels confused, numbed and unable to make any useful interpretations.

The process of thinking could be highly accelerated in group psychotherapy when a group member's particular psychopathology is driven by a compulsive need to alleviate the increasing tension, and is confronted by other group members at different stages and his condition is understood in some of its intricacies. At this point the rest of the group does the thinking. The learning by experience then is multiplied not only by the actual number of group members, but also by their own growing process of maturation which intrinsically involves the development of their own capacity to think.

Personality disordered patients do not always respond to psychotherapy; as a matter of fact, only a few do. Patients need to be adequately diagnosed. Their treatment either in individual or group psychotherapy needs to be carried out only by experienced, well trained psychotherapists and for these supervision is essential in order to function effectively.

I am referring here to the therapeutic approach which involves proper management, accurate diagnosis and being part of a working multi-disciplinary team in which cooperation of all involved is essential.

The basic point I want to put across is that the 'different diagnostic categories' do not constitute rigid, fixed cluster of symptoms to stay there forever. On the contrary, they should be understood as part of different stages of personality disorder. It is about time, as Professor Harding (1992) has strongly suggested, to stop seeing this condition as 'a totally alien process'. In trying to understand it as a process in which we all, in different degrees share, I shall taking you back to our own adolescence.

This is a particularly difficult stage when many of us felt inadequate, de-skilled and misunderstood. Explosive inner feelings and bodily changes occur at such speed that confusion sets in. The outside world appears to be neither tolerant nor patient, but actually openly hostile. During this particularly intense and painful phase we indulge in many fantasies. These serve as a means to fend against an inner experience of a hostile environment.

There are many and varied types of fantasies, from dreams of becoming a famous and intrepid astronaut to being a dangerous and equally famous gangster. Or perhaps a doctor who manages to cure all illnesses of this world to a bank robber who would be a Robin Hood and solve all poverty. Or a teacher with much knowledge who is surrounded by adoring children; or a glamorous spy who helps everybody; or a prostitute who has special gifts to make people feel better. These dreams have a kaleidoscopic quality in which a turn of 180 degrees happens in seconds. Different polarities overlap and coexist. Ethics do not count, survival does.

After a while, this role-playing fades away and is superceded by more realistically-oriented achievements. This is all part of a normative process. However, there is a group of individuals who does not follow this pattern. This normative development is unavailable to them for many and complicated reasons which I will not go into now. Instead, the dreams continue and the acting out goes on. The role-play has become a *modus vivendi*. The 'as if' quality has now acquired a pervasive quality and has become malignant self-deception. This is used as a manic defence against a chronic, masked depression, accompanied by an utter sense of emptiness and nothingness. Some individuals carry out these anti-society actions as the equivalent of a professional career.

Deception and self-deception are the key features of this condition, rarely mentioned in any description of personality disorder. These are deeply interlinked with identity confusion and the inability to see oneself from another's point of view, since the other is oneself. These two characteristics are frequently acknowledged by other authors (Akhtar 1992). A sense of false-self, accompanied by low self-esteem with an impaired capacity for thinking processes and impulsive action are present.

It is possible, as I have tried to demonstrate with my clinical vignettes that at times there are developments in some of these individuals which denote a different dynamic. This tends to appear when they are in their thirties and reveals a strong need for internal change.

A feeling of frustration emerges, some emptiness comes forward. The sense of excitement accompanying the acting out is no longer present; it has now been replaced by plain fear. The actions are now devoid of professionalism, they feel deskilled. The 'mini-kit survival' which has been used so far effectively against the black depression is no longer functioning.

We should be aware of this possibility, since it may indicate a developmental progress and a need for a move from a false-self-centred internal world to one of acknowledgement of a sense of futility and despair on themselves. This may lead to an integration with others and others' needs.

Its detection is essential and should be equated with a crucial time in the emotional growth of a child–adolescent–young adult in which an extra understanding input was needed. It requires an open mind to dynamic changes which do not always necessarily include a career of recidivism.

Acting out can easily escalate into a life of law breaking and crime and this is when we see them and assess their suitability for treatment. In the words of Gunn 'the difficulty is that in this field the concept of treatability is frequently equated with curability – which is totally inappropriate... To some extent they (personality disorders) provide the drive for the development of forensic psychiatry; medicine seems to need a separate subspecialty that will deal with behavioral disturbed people' (p.207). In my own view, forensic psychotherapy is *the* appropriate subspeciality equipped to face this therapeutic challenge.

5

Challenges to the Ambulatory Treatment Process and How to Survive Them

A Case Study

Ü. Elif Gürişik

In this chapter I will present some material from the ongoing once weekly psychotherapy sessions of a 19-year-old woman. Her diagnostic label was Munchausen by Proxy.

Winnicott (1949) suggests that the mother hates her baby before the baby hates the mother and therefore the baby knows his mother hates him. This hatred leads her to treat her baby sadistically. The professionals – paediatrician and psychiatrists alike – may be taken in by the mother's denial of her motives. However, the failure to acknowledge the mother's extreme ambivalence, hatred and murderousness, exposes both the child and the mother to further dangers by maternal acting out. The child may come to represent the unwanted aspect of the mother which the latter wants to get rid of.

When I began seeing Clare, we both had to overcome our mutual suspicion of each other. Clare, from the onset, was afraid that my interest in her was no more than my desire to set her up and trap her and eventually send her to a mental institution or prison. On the other hand I was to be taken in by her denial and to be duped. She was asking me not to make any attempt to catch her unaware, but at the same time not to be stupid enough to be duped and not to leave her at the mercy of her sadistic and murderous self. I felt I had to strike a delicate balance between these two conflicting demands.

We both had to integrate the unintegrated and digest the indigestible and find a way of working through. Also we had to overcome her persecutory anxiety, which was a definite barrier to forming a trusting working alliance. From the beginning the suffocation was an issue between us. I had to create a safe, optimal space in which neither of us felt smothered or suffocated by the other.

Daniel was referred to the Royal Brompton Hospital in 1992 by a Consultant Paediatrician in Ascot, with a history of recurrent and unexplained cyanotic episodes (in which Daniel became blue or dusky due to a lack of oxygen in the blood stream). The history was as follows:

Clinical Vignette

Daniel had five admissions to hospitals with episodes of suspended breathing. On the first admission he required mouth to mouth resuscitation and he was subsequently found to have a pneumothorax (burst lung). Prior to referral to the Royal Brompton Hospital there was a history of suspended breathing with in addition bleeding from the nose. (These are extremely unusual symptoms in infants who suffer naturally occurring apnoeic/cyanotic episodes.) At the hospitals Daniel had undergone numerous investigations, including a full screen for infectious causes, a lumbar puncture and blood culture, metabolic and electrolyte studies, and EEG to exclude an underlying problem with seizures or fits, an ultra-sound scan of the brain, ECG (heart rhythm test), chest x-ray, barium meal and coagulation screen (to pick up a bleeding tendency). All of these investigations had proved normal or negative, or failed to account for his episodes.

At the Brompton Hospital Daniel was connected to multi channel physiological monitoring and recording equipment, in order to document the changes in breathing pattern, oxygen levels, heart rate and rhythm and EEG during a typical episode. Clare had learned to use this device.

Three weeks later Daniel was readmitted to the hospital in Ascot having had a further cyanotic episode at home. Clare claimed that Daniel had been put to sleep in his car seat in the house around 10.30 am. She went upstairs to dress and a short while later, she heard the alarm of the oxygen monitor. She quickly went downstairs and found Daniel blue, not breathing and absolutely still. On further questioning she reported that Daniel was still for between one and one and a half minutes and only seemed to recover when she slapped him twice on the back. This was followed by Daniel coughing and starting to breath again. This description was inconsistent with the findings on the memory card. The pattern on the card was highly characteristic of imposed upper airway obstruction or smothering by the mother. As a result of these findings at a multi-disciplinary meeting, it was decided to use covert video surveillance to provide incontrovertible evidence to whether Daniel's episodes were natural or unnatural in origin.

On the same day Clare was seen to place both hands on Daniel's face, thereby firmly occluding his airway and Daniel was observed to struggle.

Both incidents were interrupted by the nurses. Clare was then confronted by the paediatrician and the senior sister. Clare explained that she had not meant to harm Daniel. It was explained to her that, apart from the episodes of attempted suffocation, she had indeed appeared caring for Daniel. She was then introduced to the police officers who had helped implement the covert video surveillance, and she was escorted to Chelsea Police Station.

The paediatrician felt that Daniel was at an increased risk of suffering further events, with a potential for brain injury or death. In view of this, he was separated from his mother. The paediatrician also recommended to the Court that consideration must be given to the cause of episodes that occurred to Adam, Daniel's sibling who died in June 1990. Adam was admitted to the hospital at the age of four months with gastroenteritis and convulsion. He was readmitted in the beginning of June 1990 with a history of a further convulsion. Epilepsy was diagnosed and he was commenced on phenobarbitone. Six days later he was readmitted having suffered a cardiorespiratory arrest at home. This had clearly been a major episode in that, although he was resuscitated, the post asphyxial changes resulted in him being declared brain dead in June 1990. The paediatrician suggested that Adam's episodes of reported convulsion possibly were the result of episodes of suffocation induced by the mother.

Clare cooperated with me as much as she could. However, she was not sure whether it was 'the right thing' to tell me everything as her solicitor advised her to do. She was clearly afraid that I would set her up like the paediatrician. She was still very angry with him for being instrumental in her arrests. She was aware that she found it difficult to trust people, especially doctors and psychiatrists.

From time to time she strongly protested answering some of the questions. She felt that she had been asked similar questions before and her past and present had been unnecessarily dragged up. She was anxious about being considered mad. 'Sometimes I think people think that I am mad.' She was therefore afraid that I would confirm her madness.

At the initial meeting I was struck by her half-admission and half-denial of her destructive behaviour towards her son Daniel. She pretended that she did not know the nature of her son's problems. He stopped breathing. The doctors said he had a hole in his lung. He was gasping. They said he was relapsed. I was equally struck by her incongruous affect: she displayed no emotion while describing how Adam died and what happened to Daniel. She described emptiness and depressive feelings almost cheerfully. When I pointed this out to her she objected and said that she did not want anyone to pity her. It was possible that she attempted to hide behind her smile to cover her depressive feelings. However, from time to time she totally dissociated herself from her feelings. Thus she smiled while she talked about death and depression.

The pregnancy, like the first one, was an unwanted pregnancy; 'he was not meant to be'. She first thought of having an abortion, but she could not even bring herself to think about it. She ruled out adoption after her mother's strong objections, so she decided to keep the baby.

It appears that her difficulties in looking after Daniel began soon after his birth. She perceived him as a very sickly baby with floppy muscles who 'cried all the time to play her up'. She noticed that 'Daniel did not play her mother up'. Whenever her mother picked Daniel up he became quiet. He had reflux and was allergic to dairy products. His body was covered with eczema. He had sleep disturbances as well. Soon after his birth she began to feel she was an incompetent mother who could not even hold the baby properly and could not do anything to comfort him. She sometimes felt anxious and panicky, at other times angry and depressed because she could not cope with Daniel's crying. The sleepless nights increased her resentment and anger towards Daniel. When Daniel began crying 'all she wanted was for him to shut up for five minutes'. At such times she put both her hands over Daniel's mouth and kept them there until Daniel turned blue. She then rushed out of the room in a panic and shouted for help. She stated that she wanted her mother and doctors to realize what was happening and help her to stop it, but she could not bring herself to tell anybody what she was doing to her son. She felt increasingly alone. She was afraid that if she told her mother that she was not able to cope with Daniel, her mother would make her feel stupid. 'I was always told I was stupid.'

Her father was in the Military Police. Every two years the family moved from place to place. At each move she felt uprooted. She enjoyed meeting new people, seeing new places, but she also found it nerve-racking and worrying as she wondered whether she would get on with her new friends at her new school and in the new camp.

She described her mother as a kind, loving woman, who 'will do everything for everybody'. She found her an undermining, interfering but nonetheless supportive mother who helped her to look after both Adam and Daniel, for which she felt grateful as well as resentful.

She perceived her father as completely opposite to her mother. She claimed that her father was never around when they were growing up. He never played with them, read stories, or took her or her sister to parks. She was young, she sometimes wished that she could have her best friend's father as her own father. She was very disparaging about her father when she commented: 'He cannot make a cup of tea for himself; somebody else has to do this for him'. Whenever he was around the children were asked to be quiet as he watched TV. He was the one who punished the children. He was a strict disciplinarian.

She has two sisters. One is a year older, the other four yours younger than her. She described herself as short-tempered and self-conscious as to what people thought of her, anxious about 'putting her foot in her mouth'.

As an adolescent she dressed in all black, dyed her hair black, wore lots of make up, listened to 'weird music'; and her mother called her appearance morbid. The more her mother objected to her lifestyle, her make up and her taste in music, the more she rebelled and took pleasure in rebellion.

She did not do very well at school. She had D grades in GCSEs in English, Maths, Home Economics and German.

When she met Adam's father she became pregnant very soon. However, she was not sure whether she was pregnant or not. At the time she kept worrying about her missed periods and she kept hoping that it would go away. When she decided to see a doctor, her pregnancy was already in its fifth and a half month. After her pregnancy was confirmed, she thought of abortion, but could not bear aborting a fully developed baby. She equally ruled out the thoughts of an adoption. She felt that she could not cope with the knowledge that a part of her was not there. Her mother supported her decision to have the baby and promised she would help her look after the child.

It seemed that her relationship with her boyfriend, whom she has regarded as a nasty piece of work, rapidly deteriorated. He became violent towards her; she believed that Adam's distress was caused by the beatings she took from his father. She claimed that she did not find it difficult to look after Adam, who had been described as a clinging baby. She fiercely denied that she ever attempted to harm Adam in any way.

Her association with Daniel's father began soon after Adam's death. He was always there to comfort her. She claimed that she was on the pill when she became pregnant with Daniel. 'I never forgot one single pill.' Daniel's father, like Adam's father, did not want to know anything of her pregnancy and dissociated himself from her even before Daniel was born.

When the baby was born she wanted to prove to herself that she could look after him, but she found it tough. She resented him being so needy and dependant on her. She equally resented her mother for always asking after Daniel, but failing to see that she was also in need of being looked after and taken care of.

It appeared that she had put herself in a situation in which she felt she had to prove herself as capable but she increasingly felt anxious and panicky. In turn these feelings made her feel inadequate, and by attempting to suffocate Daniel, she has wanted to get rid of the source of her distress and failure which she located in Daniel.

Seemingly she gave misleading information to her doctors about Daniel's breathing problems in order to boost her self-esteem and to be proud about her ability to deceive the hospital staff. While she was leaving the hospital with

Daniel, she kept saying to herself: 'Aren't they stupid'. However, her sense of elation did not last long. When she was faced with the same frustration and the same daily routine of looking after Daniel, she felt compelled to repeat the potentially murderous acts against him. I think that she morbidly created dramatic acts in which she was both the perpetrator and the spectator. Her lonely and dull existence came alive and was filled with caring people and excitement to which she became addicted. It is suggested that Münchausen by Proxy mothers assault their children, sometimes fatally, in order to get attention.

I would like to bring some clinical vignettes from a few sessions:

Clinical vignette

Clare began the session by saying that she did not want to come today, she felt let down, and angry. The session was very disjointed as she moved from one subject to another without elaborating. She briefly talked about her Italian tutor, the new residence in Kelly House which she found quite noisy with so many people coming and going. Her face lit up briefly as she mentioned visiting Daniel the following week. She then talked about the sitting room in Kelly House which was in a mess. She got up that morning at 06.30 am and cleaned the sitting room, but no one helped her out. By the evening the kitchen was in a disgusting state, but nobody cared, nobody bothered. It annoyed her. At the weekend she also decorated her friend's flat, that kept her busy.

She then became silent for a while, she said: 'I hate this'. She knew that she wanted to talk about a number of things, but she could not remember what they were. I suggested that she might have forgotten whatever she wanted to talk about, partly because she wanted to avoid the uncomfortable feelings they have aroused in her and partly because they might be painful to face up to. I noted that she kept herself busy with cleaning and decorating her external world and wondered whether she was trying to get away from her inner world which felt to be disgusting and messy.

I also wondered whether she felt I was like the girls in Kelly House, who did not bother helping her to clean up the internal mess. Perhaps she hated me for not helping her and for leaving her on her own at the weekend.

She said that lately she felt anxious, but she did not know why. In the past few days she had wanted to be on her own and did not want to talk to anybody (she bit her fingers). She added: 'In the last two days I have walked in a daze and felt like a zombie.' I said that by becoming like a zombie she may unconsciously be preserving me from her destructive wishes as well as getting away from her inner world, which was full of persecutors.

She responded by saying: 'I phoned my mum. My access visit was supposed to be this weekend, but mum and dad decided to visit my grandma, so my visit was postponed. Nobody told me. They arranged it with my social worker. I feel pushed out, my access visit is not counted.'

I suggested that she might be very angry with her parents and social worker for cancelling the access visit without asking her and not taking her feelings into account. She said: 'Yes, I feel very angry, I was looking forward to seeing Daniel, it was such a long time since I saw him last. My mum said I hope you don't mind, I said I have no choice, have I? Mum said you don't need to be like that and I said I was very angry. She said that they were entitled to go away. A part of me understood it. I wished that they had talked to me about the decision'.

I put it to her that she could not cope with these angry feelings and disappointments. In her attempt to suppress her rage she made herself feel like a zombie.

She said: 'I can, but when I came off the phone I was in tears, I fear Daniel is being taken away from me.' I suggested to her that she did not want to come today to her session, because she did not want to be in touch with her angry feelings and disappointment. She might have thought that I would not be bothered taking her feelings into account as well.

She said: 'I'm used to not expressing my feelings, I'm used to not going into the depth of my feelings. I am afraid that you ask more and more questions and go deeper and deeper.'

I took up her fear of deeper feelings and her wish to either obliterate her feelings by forgetting them or to anaesthetize herself against them in a daze, zombie-like state.

She said: 'When I talk about Daniel I hate myself, I didn't speak up before and that got me into trouble, but I know now I have someone I can talk to. I'm afraid of talking about my feelings and getting into trouble again and I'm afraid of getting depressed.' I said that her fear of getting in touch with her hatred and depressive feelings were stopping her from talking to me openly.

She said: 'Yes, I'm afraid how I react when I'm angry. I'm having these horrible dreams, nightmares, I dream that I am killing Daniel.' (She began to cry.) 'It is a weird dream about something else and then it jumps into another. In the last night's dream I went to mum and dad, went to bed and put my hand on Daniel's mouth and nose – I was crying as I was doing it. In the morning mum came down and asked what I had done. When I looked at Daniel, I freaked out and woke up screaming. It is a recurring dream, but it is not the same, there are some variations, but near enough the same ending.'

I said: 'I think you were expecting me to be accusatory like your mother in the dream. Persecutory, but not helpful.'

'My sister asked me the other day to hold her daughter, she was crying while her mother was getting her nappy. As I was holding the baby, I didn't feel any of those feelings which I have had when Daniel cried. I felt dizzy, anxious, I felt as if I was being watched. I would never do it ever again. It's a matter of people trusting me, I am building that trust. I'm doing what Social Services asks from me. I want to sort out my life and have a good relationship with Daniel.'

I suggested to her that her dreams were dealing with her rage, hatred and resentment towards her parents and myself, as well as Daniel.

To my surprise she said: 'I hated him! I hated him for crying, I hated him for making demands on me. I didn't want to be around him. I kept asking myself why didn't I have an abortion. When my mother informed me about the cancellation I felt very angry and, yes, the same feelings I felt towards Daniel.'

I suggested that her hatred of her parents and Daniel might also have made her feel guilty.

She said: 'I live with that guilt everyday. I feel guilty for attempting to suffocate him. I keep saying sorry to him all the time in my mind. I don't like hating my parents either. If they weren't there, Daniel would be looked after by a stranger. If they weren't there for Daniel I would have felt worse.'

I again linked being in a daze and feeling like a zombie to her powerful murderous rage, hatred and guilt arising from them. I also took up her ambivalence and dilemma in the transference. On the one hand she felt certain gratitude towards me for treating her, but not on other hand she hated me, because she needed me.

She responded by saying: 'No, I wouldn't say that. Once I hated coming here. I feel relieved when I leave here. Having you and my Probation Officer and people at the hotel make me feel supported. Before I went to the Court I felt I couldn't trust you, after the Court I was very suspicions of you. I thought you would set me up, like other doctors. I'm much more open with you now. In the last six or seven months I have talked about my feelings, like anger or hatred.'

A few weeks ago she began to talk about her recurring dream; she wakes up sweating – her dreams feel very real. She feels relieved when she realizes that she is not at her mother's house. 'I wake myself up from dreams screaming, no Clare, no Clare – trying to stop myself harming Daniel. I find it hard to go back to sleep.'

In her dreams she puts Daniel into bed, in the morning her mother looks at his cot and finds him all blue and dead. She asks: 'what have you done'? In the dream Daniel was a lot older. The house was different, it had antique furniture. Daniel cries and she attempts to comfort him and goes down stairs for a cup of coffee.

Her dreams and remembering what she had done to him, made her feel sick. 'I realize now he could have died. It is horrifying.' Then she began to talk about her first son Adam. 'There is a doubt in peoples' minds about him, I swear I never, never hurt Adam. Adam hardly cried, Daniel was a screaming baby. Adam was a contented child, he slept from nine to nine.'

'I can't blame others for thinking like that, but I am very angry with them. One thing I hate myself for is that I hadn't taken a lot of photos of him. I blamed myself after his death and kept on thinking that I wasn't a good enough mother for him, if I was a good enough mother, he would still be here. I became very depressed and didn't want to talk with anyone.'

I simply noted that she sometimes confused the names of her sons. She used Adam, Daniel interchangably. Then I suggested that in her dreams she was attempting to master the traumatic events. By dreaming her murderous attacks over and over again, she was trying to undo the damage. However, each time the dream ends up without a reparative ending. Thus the dream turns into a nightmare which can only take place in her sleep as she cannot bring herself to experience it when she is awake.

'I thought I was going mad, my mind was over playing me. I went to a spiritualist, and she said Adam was trying to show me that he was okay. It is my fault, my fault. My mum said no, it could happen to anyone, you were good with Adam. I kept saying if only, if only. The doctor told me he had idiopathic epilepsy. If he died when he was five I would have ended up in a loony bin. My younger sister was with me on the day he died, I picked him up, he was all blue and bleeding. I phoned the casualty and the police for help and ran out of the garden. I screamed: "somebody help me, help me!" No one helped me, they just looked at me. I sobbed and sobbed when I got back after burying him.'

She cancelled the next session, because she had an asthma attack. In following session she talked about her suffocating asthma attack. I drew a parallel between her asthma attack and her attempt to suffocate Daniel, and suggested to her that she might have attempted to kill off her asthmatic self, her suffering self.

She said: 'I know what one can go through if one has an attack. It is suffocating. I never thought about the asthma attack and what I did to Daniel. Shit! That little thing. What suffering I've caused. I can see, I can visualize what I put him through, but I never saw the link before. God, he must have been bloody frightened!'

As she was talking she was shaking her head from side to side and her voice was trembling. She went on: 'They say the first thing you should not do is panic, which makes breathing more difficult. Personally I wouldn't blame him if he hates me when he grows up. I can understand his hatred of me. (She began to bite her lips.) She carried on: 'They told me that he could possibly be brain damaged. I hope he's okay. I didn't think anything of being asthmatic. I just took my medicines. I know if I'm very down, depressed or anxious I get an attack.

I'm sleeping a lot better. I'm going to Milan for two weeks, working on mosaics and different styles of painting. I'm looking forward to it, but I don't know how will we will get on as a group, I've never been abroad on my own. Just, it seems so very far away.'

She went on talking about Daniel and said that she wouldn't be able to see him until she gets back from Italy. 'I talk to him on the phone every night. He knows my voice now. My mother says her eyes have to be everywhere. They've put safety things around the house. I feel a lot easier with him. That sleepless nights got me. He now sleeps through the night. He doesn't hate me though. I thought he hated me as he tried to push me away. I used to think: 'why is he doing that to me?'

I suggested that she put her hatred onto Daniel then she felt as if he hated her, in turn she hated him more than ever before. Therefore, she wanted to kill off hated and hateful Daniel to free her from her own hate and Daniel's. She responded: 'I resented him very strongly. Some days I asked myself could I go on with him another day? I did things to him on the days I resented him the most. I thought I was losing my mind, I was going mad.'

Although my presentation has mainly focused on the patient's denial of her offence, her resistance to treatment and my countertransference I hope, however, to further the discussion on whether Münchausen by Proxy as a diagnosis is helpful or even meaningful.

A nurse who murdered four children and caused severe brain damage to a number of children in her care, by administering fatal doses of insulin or potassium chloride, was diagnosed as suffering form Münchausen by Proxy. I wondered why it was difficult to call her a serial killer. Is it possible that we, the professionals, cannot bear the unbearable, to accept the unacceptable, namely the murderousness of the mother?

Calling potentially fatal acting out by mothers against their children Münchausen by Proxy is, I believe, a professional attempt to minimize, even to deny, mothers' sadism and murderousness. It must be noted that the fathers, who are charged for the similar offences, are rarely diagnosed as such.

6

Personality Disorders
The Challenge for Residential Treatment

Marijke Drost

INTRODUCTION

To whet the appetite for the subject of 'The treatment of personality disorders', I will present a case from the Dr. Henri van der Hoeven Kliniek in Utrecht. My aim is not to elaborate on the diagnostic niceties of the case, nor to focus on the psychodynamics. The idea is to offer a picture of the actual forensic practice of treating people with personality disorders. It is for the reader to decide whether this is possible or not. Much depends on the definition of the word 'treatment'. Here it will not be understood as 'cure', but as a process wherein behavioural and emotional reactions are gradually changed towards a more adequate level of functioning.

The emphasis lies on the management of the case and on the importance of teamwork. The case I have selected is not one of unmitigated failure, nor of spectacular success. It will show the trials and tribulations of both patient and therapists in a process that continues up to this very day.

Some information about the philosophy and methods of treatment in the Van der Hoeven Kliniek will be necessary to understand the background of this presentation. The outline of the patient's clinical career will be described. This is followed by a view from the individual psychotherapy. To conclude, I will point out some aspects of clinical forensic psychotherapy which seem essential to me in the treatment of personality disordered patients.

TREATMENT IN THE VAN DER HOEVEN KLINIEK

The Dr. Henri van der Hoeven Kliniek is a hospital for the treatment of persons with a so-called TBS order. This order can be given by the court in the case of offences that warrant a prison sentence of four years or more in which the perpetrator acted on the basis of a disturbed development or a mental disorder. These terms in the Dutch law encompass all sorts of disorders, including personality disorder.

The hospital is based on the principle of the therapeutic community, adapted to the forensic population for safety reasons. As much as possible, patients are stimulated to take responsibility for their own treatment; for example, to set educational or professional aims for themselves. With the help of their team they are encouraged to analyze how their feelings, attitudes and ways of reacting have led to their offence and how these patterns recur in the present.

The interactions in the group in which the patient lives are the main therapeutic instruments. These interactions are pointed out and discussed frequently by the group workers, both with individual patients and in the group. The group workers are highly qualified professionals and from different backgrounds, for example nurses, psychiatric nurses or social workers with postgraduate training. Besides the life in the group, individual psychotherapy is offered and also different problem-oriented groups with a behaviouristic and cognitive therapeutic approach.

Developing skills is an important aspect of the treatment programme. There are different workshops for professional education and preparation for the labour market outside the hospital. The education department plays an important role too. In the creative area, musical, dramatic and other skills are taught by various teachers.

Each patient has a treatment plan that is developed according to his or her central personality problems, level of education, addiction problems, and so forth. In this way there is an individualized programme of activities within the outline of the therapeutic community. The treatment plan is drawn up by a 'Head of Treatment', generally a psychologist, in close collaboration with group workers, teachers, a psychiatrist and many others. Individual or group psychotherapy may be part of the treatment plan.

OUTLINE OF THE TREATMENT'S PROGRESS

Four years ago, Miss A was sentenced to one year in prison and involuntary treatment under the TBS order. Her offence was attempted manslaughter. At the time of the offence, Miss A was addicted to hard drugs, drank a lot and worked as a prostitute.

One night she went with a customer to his house and after sexual intercourse she stabbed him several times with a kitchen knife.

Her only previous sentence had been a fine for theft. There had been no admissions to a psychiatric hospital, but she had taken part in several out-patient and clinical drug programmes.

Miss A was born into a family where both parents had had a good education and had highly qualified jobs. There is one elder sister. Miss A was a quiet child who preferred to play alone. Her early development and behaviour were unremarkable. She herself has pleasant memories of her childhood. All this is confirmed by her family.

When she was ten years old, she was told that her parents were going to get divorced. This news was totally unexpected to her. She cannot remember that she had strong emotional reactions at the time, but others report that she reacted by screaming. After the divorce, Miss A and her sister went to live with their mother. After a short time mother remarried. Miss A then began to play truant from school, started to take hashish and to have promiscuous sexual contacts. She was also involved in shoplifting. When she was absent from school, she visited bars where she met an elderly man. She made sexual advances, went with him to his house and found that his preference lay in urinating on her. She found the excitement of this adventure attractive and not at all unpleasant. Some time after this, however, she was taken home by another man. This time she remembers 'coming to' while a Moroccan man was raping her. After that other men who were present, did the same. She was turned out in the street, where she wandered confusedly about, until she met a girlfriend who took her home. Miss A thinks she was drugged by the man who took her home with him.

When she told her family what had happened, her stepfather reacted by saying that she was dirty. Miss A remembers that her mother and sister also turned away from her and she received no support whatsoever. After some months she ran away from home.

Several times she was taken to children's homes, but her behaviour remained problematic: using drugs and alcohol, running away, roaming about town and visiting bars, and going with men to find a place to stay the night.

When Miss A was fourteen years old, she started to live with a drug addicted boyfriend. This lasted for no less than seven years. He provided drugs for her, which resulted in an addiction to heroin on her part. To earn money, she started to work as a prostitute. Several attempts to become clean, failed. After the end of this relationship, Miss A was completely isolated, emotionally and socially. From this situation she committed her offence.

In 1989 Miss A is admitted to the Van der Hoeven Kliniek. She is in her late twenties at the time. Miss A does as she likes and is clearly not used to the fact that others interfere with her. She quickly establishes contacts with other patients and just as quickly drops them again. In the first month of her stay, she has sexual relations with two male patients. If the group workers try to offer structure and corrections, she reacts strongly with many conflicts. She gives up her activities very soon if she meets any frustration. This is in spite of the fact that her intelligence is well over average and she has creative talents. Her plans for study and future jobs are aimed very high and at a level far above her actual level of education. The treatment team and she have widely different opinions on this matter, which lead to many conflicts and no effective plan.

Twice she returns to her old behaviour of running away, prostitution and drug abuse. Once an affair with a patient preceded the flight. She had lent him a considerable amount of money, but he escaped from the hospital and was not heard of again. Miss A takes little initiative in exploring the reasons and dynamics of this behaviour, while any initiatives from her team get stuck in the wearisome relationship they have. An individual psychotherapist has no better results.

Miss A occupies herself a great deal with the problems of other patients, but not with her own. If she goes to see a psychotherapist at all, the contact is shortlived. She ends the visits and feels 'they do not agree together'. In this way she tries three therapists without getting anywhere.

She does not return from leave once more for a month and returns to the drug scene. In the meantime she earns some money by prostitution again. Much later it turns out that she has realized that there is nothing for her outside the hospital. Also, there nearly was a relapse of her offence. When during her work as a prostitute she felt trapped and humiliated during sexual intercourse, the thought to stab the customer crossed her mind. Because the intercourse was over soon after that, nothing happened. Feeling trapped and humiliated were the triggers for her offence in the past also.

When Miss A is back in the hospital, the team evaluates her stay up to that point. There have been three years of dodging and conflicts without any real progress. It is decided that Miss A will be transferred to a ward for intensive and individual treatment, where there is less interaction with other patients and more individual contact.

All this takes place in the autumn of 1992. I have met Miss A a month or so before her escape, with the purpose of being her next psychotherapist. The differences this time are that I am a psychiatrist and a woman. About the psychotherapy itself I will speak later on and concentrate now on the course of the clinical treatment.

Looking with a psychiatric eye, it is noticed that Miss A, among the wealth of behavioural problems, somatic complaints and feeling unpleasant generally, has developed symptoms of major depression. This becomes clearer when she is evaluated with the help of the Hamilton Rating Scale for Depression. As regards medication, she has used only sedatives up till now. After her disappointing experiences during her flight from the hospital, the diagnosis of major depression is made and she is willing to take antidepressant drugs.

In the same process of psychiatric re-evaluation her symptoms of borderline functioning are discussed with her. The things that bother Miss A herself are, among others, diffuse anxieties and possibly even micropsychotic moments of irrational fears.

The things that are noticed by others are her splitting mechanisms, instability of the self-image, of the emotional reactions and her relations. It seems useful to investigate whether a low dose of neuroleptics will help to stabilize the functioning of Miss A. She herself agrees to this. In fact, the use of neuroleptics (zuclopentixol) started some months before the antidepressant (fluoxetine).

Before the drug treatment is well under way, Miss A is transferred to the ward for intensive and individual treatment, as I mentioned before. The targets of treatment here are: learning to live without illegal drugs, realizing continuity and independent self care in daily life and gaining insight in her way of relating to others.

Miss A goes through a difficult time. She has very little energy, feels completely empty and does not know what to talk about. Yet she manages to keep up her programme of activities, although she is exhausted by eight o'clock at night. Her team invests a great deal of energy in efforts to have at least one conversation with her every day. They experience her as 'a Zombie', especially when the depression is at its worst.

Very slowly, but steadily, her condition improves. She feels that the antidepressants work out well gradually and her anxieties are greatly reduced. The weariness decreases, but the feeling of 'emptiness' persists for a long time. Others notice that she looks in better health somehow and becomes emotionally more stable and more active. The style of dress and make-up change visibly. In the past there was a preference for somewhat provocative clothes and heavy, masklike make-up. Now Miss A experiments with a more restrained style and softer colours.

Miss A takes part in a discussion group for female patients and is also an active member in a therapy group for drug addicted patients. Although she can now keep away from drugs, it is difficult to find other rewarding activities and a purpose in life.

It is striking that she is very accurate in the use of medication and makes no conflicts over it at all, in contrast to the past when sedatives were prescribed. Twice the dosage of neuroleptics is slightly reduced and both times the anxieties and micropsychotic moments return after a couple of days. So it is decided to continue a fixed dosage for a long time.

The progress is such that Miss A can return to her former group gradually. Once there, she manages to keep to her plans, which are not to take the problems of others on herself and to keep away from sexual relationships. She fears that she will lose her own identity again if she becomes too close to others, especially within a sexual relationship. When the man to whom she has lent so much money is found by the police and possibly will return, she becomes nervous and fearful. She realizes that she only seems stabilized, but that everything is fragile really and she will not be able to withstand the man in direct confrontation.

Meanwhile her condition is such that a transfer to a sheltered housing project elsewhere becomes possible. She is no longer emotionally unstable or inactive, looks after herself and her finances well and she has started to broaden her contacts outside the hospital. For example, the relationship with her family is re-established and she visits her relatives sometimes. Also she takes lessons in yoga and aerobics in town. Miss A goes to these lessons alone and always returns at the agreed time.

In the period that the transfer becomes an actual reality because Miss A becomes no. 1 on the waiting-list, she suddenly brings alcohol in a lemonade bottle into her room and drinks it all. This is occasioned by 'boredom', she says. Two weeks later she does not come back for her aerobic lessons, but turns to drugs and prostitution again for two days. She then returns to the hospital of her own accord. It becomes clear that she has started a sexual relation with a male patient who has a girlfriend elsewhere. As the relationship has no perspective, she has manoeuvred in such a way that she is emotionally trapped and she has to flee to set herself free.

INDIVIDUAL PSYCHOTHERAPY

The first aim is to establish a working relationship with Miss A and to get continuity in her visits to the therapist.

This is done by 'being there' in a supportive way and by offering a structured meeting where the therapist is active in proposing the subjects of discussion. Although Miss A wants to understand more about her past, she remembers very little material about her childhood. This worries her. A list of topics for discussion is drawn up. Some of the items are: looking through her book of family snapshots, the rape experience, relationships with men, her medication programme.

In an unstructured interview it is very difficult for Miss A to fill the time. She can discuss facts and memories, also how she feels at the moment, but there is little insight on a deeper level. Her mood swings from hypomanic to anhedonia. When at her request the length of the interviews is reduced to thirty minutes a week, she feels more relaxed. The relationship with the therapist becomes continuous after some conflicts in the beginning. For Miss A one of the main reasons is that her own story is central in the contact and the therapist does not bring in bits of information from other sources, such as what the team say about her. Also she apparently trusts a psychiatrist more than a psychologist.

With a female therapist, Miss A feels more free to discuss her sexual experiences. At first she brings up the memories of the rape episode; later on she talks about the way she totally devoted herself to a partner to please him and thus to feel worthwhile and well liked. When the therapist carefully asks about the possibility of incest in her past, Miss A considers this in an almost clinical way, without expressing any emotions, but she does not remember anything of the sort. She feels no desire to try and find out. Many sessions are devoted to making a scenario of the events, thoughts and feelings immediately preceding her offence. From this story high risk situations are identified. A list of warning signs and a prevention plan are drawn up. In relation to the discussion of her fears and instability, much attention is paid to psychoeducation about vulnerability, the need to have order in her life, and so on.

On the intellectual level Miss A is interested and works along these lines in her daily life. Emotionally she remains insecure. In contrast with the past, she now is aware of this insecurity, which frightens her. She no longer blames everything on others or acts out with her former self-destructive behaviour.

In the phase where her team discusses the sheltered housing project with her, Miss A at first is happy to go there. She feels she needs a new phase in her development to crown her efforts up till now. Her emotional reactions are more confused: first she is very nervous when the man who has swindled her of her money, almost returns; then she turns to alcohol 'from boredom'; then she runs away to drugs and prostitution again. Only just before that the topic in psychotherapy had been how she wanted to relate to men. Just friends and no sex, she said. If she were to start having sex with someone, she doubted if she could avoid fusion with that person. The problem was that she already felt sexually attracted to a particular patient and said she wanted to keep her distance nevertheless. She did not tell the therapist that she did have sexual intercourse with him. Some sessions later Miss A suggests that she herself needs different deviant varieties of sex, because they give her a feeling of pleasant sensation – to be picked up by a customer, when anything may happen.

COMMENT

The case I have discussed here is that of a young woman who conforms to the criteria of borderline personality disorder according to DSM III-R. Also Kernberg's three aspects of borderline organization can be distinguished: an unstable sense of self, use of primitive defence mechanisms and temporary lapses in reality testing.

The development of Miss A took a wrong turn after the sudden divorce of her parents. Although her history is suggestive of sexual abuse in childhood, no more insight is gained in that area. Miss A herself sees the divorce as the start of the troubles and has no wish to explore otherwise. Besides, she says, she remembers very little of her childhood. This amnesia in itself may cover traumatic experiences. The general anhedonia, the tendency to feelings of derealization and the powerlessness against intrusive sexual experiences may also be interpreted as late effects of trauma.

Be that as it may, after the start of the conduct disorder, Miss A very quickly and at a young age, went astray in all areas of life. She only made an attempt to pick up her development fourteen years later.

During the clinical treatment, a diagnosis of comorbidity with depression was made and treated separately. Other comorbidity, such as substance use, was noticed too. This was attended by special group therapy for addicted patients. The educational and professional achievement were greatly improved. Individual psychotherapy ran through all the years of treatment, although discontinuous at first. The progress there lagged behind the results in other areas.

RELEVANT FACTORS IN THE TREATMENT
OF PERSONALITY DISORDERS

Many characteristics of this patient, however, are also present in forensic patients with other types of personality disorder. To mention a few: low achievement, impulsivity, disturbed close relationships, a tendency to addiction, paranoid ideation or a general feeling that others mean harm and constitute danger to oneself. The patients tend to act out their conflicts instead of developing symptoms. Their inclination to introspection is limited. In the case of forensic patients, they only remain in therapy because the staff takes a lot of trouble to motivate them and because there is no getting away from the therapeutic environment.

The story of Miss A is by no means exceptional for the patients who are treated in the Van der Hoeven Kliniek. The different approaches that are taken to her treatment apply also to other patients with personality disorders.

Let me point out some aspects of the treatment which seem relevant to me for treating personality disordered patients in general.

1.   The start takes a long time. The patient does not want to be in the hospital, and has often no sense of having a problem. Basic trust is often absent. Therefore much time and energy has to be spent on motivating the patient and getting him or her used to the daily routines that offer structure and predictability. In short, establishing a working alliance is problematic, for the treatment team as well as for the individual therapist.

2.   Earlier patterns of behaviour with the attendant danger of recidivism remain present for a long time, even if there is superficial adaptation and progress. An estimation of how much things have really changed will not be found out through individual therapy alone, but will be

seen in the actual behaviour of the patient in the group where he or she lives, or during visits into society.

3. Gunderson and Kolb (1978), among others, point out that the low level of work and school achievements is a major problem for borderline patients, and I would like to add for other types of personality disordered patients as well. They stress the role that social learning programs, like groups, rehabilitation and the therapeutic environment, can have in comprehensive treatment planning.

   In the case presented, we see the different approaches that were applied in the treatment plan of this particular patient. There was a change from a group with high interaction levels to a ward with individual care and back again. Individual psychotherapy formed a part of the larger treatment plan. Education and work were continuous influences to strengthen the ego-functions. All these different areas of therapeutic influence fertilize each other. Some will support the Ego-strength and improve the patient's intellectual grasp on unintelligible feelings. Others support the self-image by providing a role in the group or a professional identity. In continuous confrontation and explanation, the patient can learn that there is something like 'feelings' or that other people also have them.

4. Social skills often are very underdeveloped in the patients. Some cannot refuse demands from others. They may understand that this has to do with fear of rejection, but this alone will not improve their skills. Others can never comply with someone else's demands, because that would mean annihilation for them. The training of practical skills to deal with others in certain situations should be a standard item in the treatment program.

5. In certain cases the use of medication is to be considered. Personality disorder generally often overlaps with DSM-III-R's Axis I symptoms. In our population mood disorders, usually masked depression, are a regular feature. There are also reports that a slight dose of neuroleptics can be helpful, with the borderline patient as well as with other types of personality disorder. Medication should be seen as a means of controlling disabling symptoms in the context of an overall treatment plan that includes individual, group, family and behavioural therapy.

CONCLUSION

All approaches to the treatment of personality disordered patients have at least three features in common (adapted from Shea 1991). First, careful attention has always to be paid to the establishment of a trusting and collaborative relationship with the patient. Second, the therapist plays an active role, is supportive and sets limits to impulsive behaviour. Third, it is important to select reasonable goals of treatment. How much improvement can be expected? Up till now, no convincing research on the outcome of distinct therapeutic approaches is available, let alone that one theoretical framework is clearly superior to others. Therefore an eclectic approach seems most appropriate at present.

In the long experience of the TBS system in general, it is found anyway that many patients can be released from the forensic hospital and continue on a better and less damaging level of functioning than before their admission. Although complicated and time consuming, the treatment of personality disorders is possible and rewarding.

Especially in the forensic field, the results are many, not only for the patient and his or her social network, but also to the society in general in so far as there is a decrease the chances of dangerous behaviour. As this behaviour was the reason for the admission in the first place, this result of treatment is not to be despised. Psychotherapy after all does not take a place in a vacuum, but in a social context.

7

The Action Film 'Terminator' – Gateway to Aggressive Fantasies in Adolescence?

Reinmar du Bois

Most delinquent adolescents who are proposed for treatment have committed some sort of aggressive act. The question whether we shall find a therapeutic approach to these young people refers to doubts as to whether we shall be able to understand their aggressiveness. If we take our task lightheartedly, we can try to explain their aggression as due to an excess of aggressive libidinous energy adding the Freudian theory of death instinct, supplemented by the assumption of a traumatic childhood and an element of biological vulnerability. This concept could of course be further elaborated and perfected by pointing out the modern estrangement and manipulation mechanisms prevalent in today's living conditions and social norms.

It would be pointless to pursue this concept any further, as it cannot easily be transformed to the more clinical issues of aggressive personality disorders, let alone to therapeutic action. I would therefore like to present two short case examples, which I will not describe in detail, as they are only to recall some of the 'flavour' of aggressive behaviour in such personality disorders.

The first case is that of the 20-year-old Drago. As an infant he grew up with his grandparents in Croatia, then with his parents in Germany, where two younger siblings were born. The family climbed up the social ladder, but his mother became a secret alcoholic. From puberty onwards he was a frequent truant from school. He roamed around and suffered from lack of social contact. His parents, especially the mother, kept bashfully secret that the son was a bully at home and terrorized and sometimes attacked both his parents. Next door lived an 80-year-old single lady. Drago often helped her in her garden and repeatedly intruded into her house to steal money and other valuables. The old lady became suspicious and reported to the police without mentioning his name. One night Drago wanted to get himself a bottle of champagne from her cellar. He had vague ideas with whom he might celebrate and empty the bottle. Instead of climbing in secretly as he had always done before, he made noises and even rang the doorbell, as he said, in order to distract the lady's attention. He then stayed in the basement for much too long, until the lady came downstairs and saw him. He killed her by choking, undressed her lower parts and masturbated between her legs.

The second example is that of the 17-year-old Jan. He had a trivial argument with his mother about pocket money and payment for a ticket for a football match. The mother withdrew herself, as she had to go to work. Subsequently Jan went off to the football stadium. There were some quarrels between two rivalling fan groups, but no severe fighting, and Jan was only marginally involved. He was slightly angry that his group had not insisted and fought back. On the way home in the electric train, it somehow struck him that the man sitting opposite himself was looking at him in a peculiar way. The man carried a briefcase. It suddenly occurred to him that the case might contain a weapon. He seized the man's jacket, shook him and hit him in the face. He found it strange that the man did not fight back at all and that eventually blood poured out of his nose. The more passively the man behaved, the more he felt provoked. He continued to beat until the man sank to the floor, and even then he had to be dragged away by his friends, who urged him to flee.

These cases illustrate some issues of aggressiveness in young disturbed people as they will inevitably reiterate in all therapeutic work.

1.   The aggressive acts flare up instantaneously and are seemingly unprovoked.

2.   The aggressive acts can progress to micropsychotic states of excitement and imminent loss of reality and affect control.

3.   The aggressive acts give rise to the assumption that they are accompanied and supported by vivid fantasies, which have long been formed before the acts and persevere long afterwards.

4.   In all such aggressive acts we see emanations of traumatized mother–child relationships and the attempted defence of homosexual and incestuous wishes.

The validity of these psychoanalytical views on aggressive personality disorders is beyond dispute. I am, however, aiming beyond the scope of theoretical reasoning. I am mainly concerned about the technical question of how one can proceed from here toward successful psychotherapeutic action. Every experienced therapist knows how painful it may be for both sides to face the ugliness of aggressive fantasies and to establish a transference relationship on this basis. Moreover, treating pathological aggression is often like walking in a dry river bed in the desert. The conversations are deprived of all imagery and the flow of feelings is totally blocked, until suddenly a torrent of such fantasies along with a negative transference reaction threatens to destroy the therapeutic process. We often find that aggressive fantasizing is effectively blocked, not only during the sessions, but throughout the patient's conscious life, until the next aggressive outburst occurs.

My therapeutic attempts with the above mentioned patients had a curious commonality. Both patients had seen the film 'Terminator' and 'Terminator 2', not only once, but several times and urged me to share their views about these films with me. They were both deeply acquainted with the scenes and imagery of the films. They implored me to see the films myself or even watch them in their company.

Here is a brief outline of the plot of the first of the two films.

One day in our time two naked creatures fall down to the earth in artificial showers of lightning. One of them is crouched down and cramped together in pain, as if he has just been born. At once he gets into danger and has to run for his life. The other, who lands somewhere else, stands upright and unharmed, calm and unimpressed and pursues his task. This creature is a robot made from metal covered with a deceptive layer of skin and flesh, in perfect human shape. Both creatures have arrived from the future to our present age in order to look for a particular woman. Her son, who has not even been conceived, is going to become the future leader in their world, a messenger of hope in a hopeless world. In this future world human rebels are fighting against superior robots. Flashbacks lead into this repulsive world. It has an apocalyptic and darkened scenery of wrecks and ruins, the leftovers of a worldwide atomic disaster. The surviving humans live miserably under the surface of the earth – starving and dying. They are hunted by the machines and will eventually be extinguished.

The Terminator, a technologically most advanced and humanlike machine, has been programmed to kill the female hero. She is totally unsuspecting. Her killing is designed to wipe out the existence of the future leader before his life has even begun. The male human opponent to the Terminator has also been sent down from the future. His task is of course to save the woman. He sacrifices himself and is killed towards the end of the film, leaving it to the woman to neutralize the robot. Before the final showdown there is time for just one brief sexual encounter, and thus the future rebel leader is conceived. The film ends when the pregnant woman, who has matured under the strain of her ordeal, tries to drive her car way from the imminent atomic disaster. There is something heroic and triumphant about her, as she faces her fate, being the mother of a future leader.

Everything is impinged with hopelessness. But the woman remains the grandiose projection screen for pain, anxiety, sexual lust, fantasies of incest, birth and rebirth. In a deeper sense this woman is the origin of almost everything in the film, the starting point and the finishing point for all the atrocities. The film is uncompromisingly brutal and violent. Everything is legitimated by an inescapable nemesis. The humans are subjected to their lot which they cannot change. Yet they are fighting back. Even though they conceive themselves as victims, they engage themselves as warriors. Behind the highly aggressive pitch of the film there is a secret desire for regression, gratification and passive surrender lurking in the background. It is never made open, yet it can be sensed throughout the film.

Based on this description my first hypothesis concerning aggressive fantasies in young people suggests that they are transporting strong wishes for passive surrender and regression. This is accomplished by constructing a nearly metaphysical and religious perspective.

Let us consider a few more film sequences. The Terminator arrives at the reception desk of a police station and asks for the woman. There is a listless and tired officer, who is busy with some paper work, telling the Terminator – without looking up that he should wait at a bench in the corner. The Terminator remarks bluntly that he will not wait, but return. A few seconds later a car crashes right into the room and the wall bursts to pieces. Then the Terminator starts shooting himself a passage through the building killing everyone who crosses his path.

This scene shows that at least some aggressive fantasies inside and outside such films centre around sudden eruptions which occur unexpectedly and straight out of sleepiness and boredom. This important pattern of imagination should warn us to disregard or belittle boredom as an emotional state of no significance. The scene where boredom turns into rage, reminds us of the close interaction between these two states, i.e. between rest and excitation, harmlessness and danger. The element of surprise leaves the victim no chance. There is hardly any trace of a search for contact or a human encounter, which we can observe in some other aggressive acts. The scene is reduced to an abreaction. Neither aggressor nor victim take any chance to become aware of or control the act.

Thus my second hypothesis concerning the nature of pathological aggression fantasies implies that they contain an ambivalent wish for loss of control. These fantasies may be derived from unsuccessful experiences of masturbation and orgasm. Inhibitions of orgasmic and masturbatory activity are, by the way, not infrequently observed in young patients with a pathological aggression problem.

In a further scene of the film the viewer discovers that the police do not have the slightest idea about the severity of the danger around them. The police make ignorant and ridiculous offers to help. But obviously the protagonists of the film will have to look after themselves. There is some schizoid and autistic thinking in this. Each fighter is completely alone. He cannot count on any external help. Many adolescent delinquents experience themselves just like that. Being unable to come to terms with the world they add a touch of grandiosity to their isolation, thus making it more tolerable. As they refuse any help, they avoid the embarrassment of being confronted with their own weakness.

Towards the end of the film there is a chase on highways and in a steel plant. The Terminator has several gruesome accidents and is gradually dismembered and distorted. But he remains dangerous till the very last moment. The attempts to kill the robot are stepped up in a way that is hard to bear.

Finally the woman is all alone and manages to crush him under a steel press. From this film material we can conclude that aggressive fantasies contain loops and endless repetitions. Fantasies of violence must be replayed until they have reached a limit of emotional tolerance. The aggressive behaviour is persecutory, it is relentless and never ending. At least the film suggests that some aggressive persons are caught in scenarios of attack and danger and cannot escape. These scenarios constitute a basic existential feeling of compulsion in some of our young patients.

I am now proceeding to another film sequence. In their attempts to escape from the Terminator, the woman and her male guard hide in a sort of shelter. There the male hero tells the woman about his secret bond tying him to her through time and space. In his world he had once possessed a polaroid picture of her. It was burnt in a fire blast, but he managed to keep her image in his mind.

Here at last a sort of relationship between the man and the woman is admitted and psychologically focused in the film. But the sequence is extremely short. Yet it is the object of endless speculations by my patients. The male hero clings to the picture of an idealized female person – undoubtedly a mother figure. She is in fact the only surviving individual at the end of the film and the one who overcomes the robot. Moreover she will deliver a child which will survive the virtual end of the world.

All my patients have idealized the female in this film to the highest degree. They have done so despite the fact that she is depicted in an ambiguous role: on the one hand she is subjected to the worst persecution – enough to suffer from psychic trauma till the end of her life. On the other hand the future robots know only too well that any real danger will originate just from this female figure and her creative and destructive potential. Behind the idealization there is a knowledge that the woman is also the source of the aggressive fantasies.

It is no coincidence that in all successful horror films the mother figures play a vital role inviting and encouraging young men to violent action. Against this background it may be argued that the mother figure does not really need protection, but the male figures should rather seek to protect themselves.

Without the antagonism of a good male hero the film plot would contain nothing but an endless nonsensical persecution of a woman. To what atrocity the woman is really able to proceed, can be discovered in the final scene, when she finishes the Terminator by pressing a button. This act resembles an execution or – more daringly – a grandiose castration.

The sexual aspect of the man to woman relationship is shown most sparingly. It is probably far too dangerous to give more room to sexual experiences in such a dangerous environment. There is only one short film sequence, where the man and the woman arrive at a motel on their flight from the Terminator. There they engage themselves building explosive devices. Then suddenly a passionate sexual encounter takes place, but hardly any tenderness is shown. The sexual act is all breathlessness and excitement. Two hands are clasped together in a spasm, which is shown in a close-up.

This scene conveys the message that sexual love is associated with the highest degree of danger and can only be performed out of extreme situations, out of the same situations in fact, which can be life-threatening. There is little difference. The sexual arousal is derived from an anxiety tinged battle state. Aggressive and sexual excitement merge into each other. All relations between men and women are close to such amalgamation fantasies and are thus only tolerable for a very short time. The sexual act does not grant the full relaxation which Ferenczi has always demanded.

In my talks with my patients about this film, it was first of all the grandiosity of the violent scenes that had caught their imagination. Second, they were attracted by the gloomy role of the male hero.

Meanwhile my repertoire of understanding this film has increased: remember the beginning of the film, when two naked beings descended from nowhere in the dark of the night and at once began to search for the same woman with the utmost intensity and determination, one with 'good', the other with 'evil' intentions. Both men are the offspring of the same apocalyptic world. They appear as opponents, but they are possibly the only two sides of the same fantasy, which is directed towards the woman. These fantasies are immensely dangerous. In order to suppress the sexual wishes towards a mother figure, she must be destroyed. In the end the woman turns into a hero and a saint.

I tend to view the whole murderous persecution of the woman as a defence against homosexual wishes. In many ways the two men, one a robot and one a weak human, are related to each other. They may even look for each other. They get killed at almost the same time. They are both on a search for the same woman and they do not succeed. Possibly one of the many fascinations of the film is this element of concealed homosexuality.

But there are many other fascinations. The film offers many opportunities to negotiate dynamic aspects of violent fantasies, that can otherwise not be directly targeted. The fantasies are both revealed and disguised as they remain fictional, not factual. Some may be afraid that the film material might place an obstacle for the real fantasies of a patient to come to the fore or might divert or pervert them out of all recognition. This is not so. Of course the film material is a challenge for the patient as he tries to form his own identity. The Terminator fantasies are, however, half way between the patient's self and the film as a separate entity. My patients have entered into a most intensive dialogue with the contents of the film and have thus been able to clarify their own emotional insides.

My initial resistance and even aversion against the film and its manneristic and violent message have meanwhile diminished. I reckon that it had mainly irrational sources and that I was merely afraid of confronting myself with the full extent and scope of aggressive fantasies in my patients.

Whenever my patients make reference to the Terminator, their aim is to clarify their own fantasies, but at the same time to seal off some other aspect, which may still be too dangerous to disclose or to become fully aware of. The Terminator fantasy closes a gap and serves as a temporary substitute.

Based on these experiences so far, I would cautiously recommend accepting this film and similar films in our therapeutic work, provided they are offered by the patients themselves during the sessions.

Based on the Terminator fantasies it may then be possible for both sides to gain a common understanding of the destructive potential of all sexual arousal, the intensity of the longing for the lost maternal object and intensity of the fear to lose control. I have learnt to share with patients a better understanding of the proximity of sexual and criminal fantasies, and to understand the compulsion which is exerted by fantasies of persecution and revenge. Even the hopelessness of the heros in the film is finally transformed into triumph. Similarly, in view of all the suffering, it seems to be a sort of comfort that someone like a robot, who looks like a human, can receive the deepest wounds without feeling the appropriate pain.

8

Residential Forensic Treatment

The Interplay Between Case Management and Institutional Management

Henri Wiertsema and Frans Derks[1]

INTRODUCTION

In this chapter we will analyze two levels of organizational management of forensic treatment. The first is case management of individual treatment programmes; the other is institutional management, including internal and external security. Quality is based on their interdependence. We will deal with the following topics:

- o the institutional goals of forensic psychiatry
- o the treatment principles of the Van der Hoeven Kliniek
- o the organizational aspects of case management and
- o institutional management, including internal and external security.

In the final section we will generalize individual and institutional management aspects to social policy problems at the national level.

INSTITUTIONAL GOALS

Forensic psychiatry is a medical discipline and a juridical instrument at the same time. Its task is to integrate treatment with security. Residential forensic

---

1 A slightly modified version of this paper has been published in *Therapeutic Communities; International Journal for Therapeutic and Supportive Organisations* (1994), 15; 247–254.

treatment centres offer treatment to patients who lack motivation and whose behaviour in an uncontrolled setting is potentially dangerous. The institutional goal is reduction of the probability of reoffending. Thus management teams of residential forensic treatment centres must provide for:

- the *definition* of treatment principles
- the *formulation* of an organizational-therapeutic philosophy
- the *transformation* of philosophy into treatment facilities and general programs and
- 'tailor-made' *application* of facilities and programs in each individual case.

Therapeutic quality is based on the general philosophy and its translation into interdependent programmes and facilities. For patients and personnel it must be clear that programmes and facilities are derived from general therapeutic principles.

TREATMENT PRINCIPLES

In the final instance the goal of treatment is to prevent reoffending. Treatment is future-oriented. For each individual patient there will come a moment when involuntary residential treatment ends. The task of treatment teams therefore is to assist the patient in finding a new place in society. He must develop the skills needed to maintain his position in the community without offences against other people. After treatment the patient will return into his own world of daily social interactions with relatives, friends, colleagues and others. Treatment must not only focus on the individual, but also on his social situation after treatment.

Even though the therapeutic environment in the treatment centre is by definition artificial, the differences with the 'normal' social situation in the community must be kept to a minimum. If treatment aims at resocialization, the patient has to learn skills to live in the community. These skills must be practised while under treatment: in the centre and in the community.

The centre offers a controlled and secure environment. It is only to a limited degree that treatment results can be assessed under these controlled conditions. There should be the opportunity to assess progress in real life situations within the community. For this reason, supervised community living while under treatment is an indispensable part of the total process. What can be done in the community should not be done inside the forensic treatment centre. One should not create and apply for the forensic patients treatment facilities which are available to them in the community. For security reasons, this obviously requires frequent and strict supervision of the patient's behaviour outside the hospital.

The fact that the patient has committed a serious crime does not imply total incapacity to behave in a socially responsible manner. Forensic patients tend to externalize their problems; they give us the impression that they are not motivated for treatment. But at the same time they know that their behaviour has been inadequate. Some of them have previously tried to change their behaviour, but they lacked assistance and were unable to sustain in their effort. Externalization has become their 'survival strategy'. This implies that medical, social and personality shortcomings must be identified, but they should not be the exclusive focus of treatment. Forensic treatment not only aims at unlearning negative behaviour, but also at the strengthening of positive skills.

CASE MANAGEMENT

The continuation of external social relations during residential treatment is of special therapeutic importance. The analysis and therapeutic processing of family relations, friendships and instrumental relations are essential for rehabilitation. In the individual case this requires continuous evaluation of therapeutic opportunities offered by external social relations on the one hand, and security requirements on the other. For example, even if the treatment goal is to develop an external social network, we must prevent friendships with persons who might keep the patient in a criminal environment.

Patients have shortcomings, but they also have positive abilities. Sometimes their shortcomings are in the foreground, sometimes the positive skills. After treatment the patient will be held responsible for his own behaviour in less controlled conditions than in the treatment centre. This is why at the Van der Hoeven Kliniek he is given as much responsibility for his treatment as possible. Right from the start patients are stimulated to take this responsibility. Each patient is involved in the making of his own treatment plan. He must commit himself to the goals formulated in the plan. This requires a therapeutic approach in which the formulation of realistic goals and a confrontation with their shortcomings motivate patients to make use of treatment facilities. The controlled treatment setting helps them to sustain in this effort, where they previously failed.

From the institutional goal of prevention of reoffending it follows that treatment aims at behavioural changes in the first place. Treatment is not contained in any specific therapeutic activity which is offered on an exclusive theoretical basis. Treatment is the educational orchestration of normal social interactions. The therapeutic environment is organized in such a way that patients experience the consequences of their behaviour in day-to-day living situations. Patient–staff and patient–patient interactions within the living group form the nucleus of the treatment process.

To support sociotherapy several educational and therapeutic programs are being offered. Depending on the individual treatment plan, these may range from schooling and job training to creativity training and physical education. In the plan, there must be a balance between socio- and psychotherapy, job training, schooling and other activities. This balance differs from person to person, because their shortcomings and capacities differ.

At the individual level 'tailor-made' treatment plans and programmes require a realistic treatment goal and a clear structure. When the goal is too high, we do not offer the patient a realistic perspective; if it is too low, he will not become motivated to change. When the structure is too loose there is insufficient control, but when it is too rigid we do not stimulate the patient to develop his capacities. In each individual case it must be decided whether treatment should focus on the patient's abilities or on his disabilities. Patients may have specific skills which offer a clue for therapeutic intervention, but their disabilities may be so prominent that these must be tackled first (e.g. current addiction, psychotic disintegration, or aggressive acting-out). This requires assessment of motivation, security requirements, skills and shortcomings – for example assessment of psychiatric symptoms, social skills and cognitive abilities. Psychotic patients, for example, require a different balance in their programme than personality disordered patients. They need more 'care' and less 'confrontation'.

INSTITUTIONAL MANAGEMENT

Questions at the institutional level are related to those at the case level, but they are of a different order. One obvious institutional problem is posed by the variety of treatment plans and programmes that results from the individualized approach. Their diversity demands coordination at the institutional level. But we also need high quality personnel, who are able to work in interdisciplinary cooperation.

Institutional management is not a goal in itself, but is secondary to behavioural change as the goal of treatment at the case level. Both have the same objective; they are interdependent. From a therapeutic perspective, to learn a profession may greatly increase the patient's chances for successful community living. But we also have an institutional profit from the work that the patients do in the job training departments.

In the hospital kitchen, for example, two professional cooks are assisted by a number of patients who are responsible for the preparation of daily meals for the total hospital population. This yields an institutional profit in terms of reduced personnel. An additional profit is that the kitchen is not only a kitchen, but also a therapeutic instrument. The cooks are not only cooks, but also therapeutic personnel. For the patients who work in the kitchen, they are part of the treatment team. The same is true for all the other services in the hospital, such as administration, domestic services, gardening, etc. Mutual profit and shared responsibility are the crux of staff–patient cooperation.

As far as security management is concerned, one must differentiate between *internal* and *external* security. As regards external liberties the personnel is exclusively responsible for any decision. But at the Van der Hoeven Kliniek things are different as regards internal security. Internal security, in physical terms as well as in psychological ones, is a precondition for any therapeutic process to develop. In these matters, personnel and patients have a common interest; this is a shared responsibility. This notion of shared responsibility creates a therapeutic, non-repressive atmosphere which allows for the absence of specialized security personnel. Security problems and other violations of the therapeutic climate are solved in cooperation between staff and patients. The problem is defined as a problem of the total hospital community, including the patients. Again the kitchen may serve as an example. In September and October 1993 the kitchen was out of use, because of a large renovation. This problem was discussed with the patients. We proposed to get meals from an external catering company, but the patients preferred to cook their own meals in the living groups. At this moment, a number of groups still cook for themselves, even though they could get their meals from the renovated kitchen. Thus, the *problem* was shared, the *solution* was shared and the *responsibility* was shared.

Resocialization as the goal of forensic treatment is inconsistent with any partition of the treatment process into a number of successive and relatively independent stages (such as an admission phase, a treatment phase and a resocialization phase). If resocialization is the goal of treatment, this goal must be pursued right from the start. We do not believe in a stage-model of treatment.

We have specialized wards for psychotic patients and for individual treatment, but their specialization is not based on a stage-model. We have learned that an institutional structure of separate intake, treatment and resocialization wards is inadequate for forensic treatment of personality disordered patients.

More than ten years ago we attempted to create a ward for patients who already had work in the community. This was not a success. A smooth internal flow and the flow into the community were blocked. The same would be true for an intake ward. New patients are admitted into groups of patients who already know the therapeutic climate. They are easily introduced in the centre's culture. They are motivated by other patients to utilize the therapeutic facilities. If necessary, other patients confront them with their reluctance to be personally responsible for their own treatment.

A final organizational characteristic of the Van der Hoeven Kliniek is the emphasis on personnel as the most important therapeutic instrument in a forensic context. The centre's therapeutic standard largely depends on the quality of the personnel and on the theoretical and practical expertise of each employee. The organization must stimulate application of their knowledge in cooperation with other disciplines. For this reason, we do not have much personnel, but we prefer to have good educated employees instead.

Interdisciplinary cooperation requires a collective goal and the awareness that each discipline makes its own contribution to this goal. The collective goal is to resocialize each patient as quickly as possible. Each individual employee must identify himself with this goal.

A strong hierarchical structure would frustrate this identification. For this reason the organizational structure of the Van der Hoeven Kliniek is as flat as possible. It may be obvious that in final instance the board of directors is responsible for treatment and security, but there is a minimum of intermediate organizational levels. Identification with the institutional goal is stimulated by an emphasis of collective responsibility for reaching the goal at the case level. Differences between disciplines are based on their different contributions to the treatment process as a whole.

One other precondition for collective responsibility is that all relevant information is shared. The relatively low number of employees facilitates the sharing of information. At the Van der Hoeven Kliniek no employee has more information about a patient than any other employee. Structured exchange of information between disciplines is vital for the treatment of personality disorders. The organizational basis is the daily staff meeting, in which the total hospital staff participates and where decisions regarding individual patients are made by the collective staff. This daily meeting forms the basis of collective responsibility and the collective goal.

CONCLUSION

Let us try to generalize these institutional principles to the national level. We are, in our opinion, currently faced with two basic social policy problems. First, a practical problem in terms of insufficient capacity of the forensic treatment system. And second, an ideological problem in terms of punishment versus treatment.

Current capacity of the forensic treatment centres in The Netherlands is not sufficient to absorb the increasing number of personality disordered criminal offenders. According to recent estimates, we need at least a hundred extra beds in the residential treatment system. One obvious answer to this problem is to build additional treatment centres. But a more economic solution may be to increase the output of the forensic treatment system by means of an accelerated transfer of patients to non-forensic facilities. This, however, would require close cooperation between the departments of Justice and Public Health at the national level, as well as between forensic and non-forensic treatment centres at the local level.

In addition, treatment centres must try to shorten the period of residential treatment and to extend the period of supervised community living. This too would increase the residential capacity. Recent calculations have shown that a reduction of residential treatment by six months would create seventy to eighty additional places in the forensic treatment system.

As far as differences between punishment and treatment of offenders are concerned, it is our view that one must not try to treat and punish simultaneously. Treatment of personality disordered criminal offenders requires specialized treatment centres, which are organized according to *therapeutic* principles – not *punishment* principles. The arguments in favour of treatment of personality disorders in the prison system are not valid. Acute psychiatric symptoms can obviously be treated in a prison setting, but personality disordered patients require a different regime.

In terms of their goals there is a fundamental difference between treatment and punishment. The goal of punishment is retaliation; the goal of treatment is resocialization. This must be expressed in separate organizational structures, regimes, personnel and facilities. Treatment of personality disorders requires a therapeutic climate, not a repressive one. Therapeutic quality of forensic psychiatry can only be ensured in a forensic treatment system separate from the national prison system.

9

Treating Psychopaths in England

Donald West

British clinicians have become increasingly cautious about taking on responsibility for treatment of socially deviant behaviours. Fifty years ago psychiatric hospitals were authoritarian institutions in which inmates locked away and subjected to prison-like regimes, where control and discipline were in greater evidence than efforts to communicate with patients. Psychiatric decisions on compulsory detention were rubberstamped by magistrates and went largely unchallenged. Sometimes women of near normal intelligence, but with inconvenient promiscuous sexual habits, were shut away in asylums for years under provisions of the 1927 Mental Deficiency Act as supposed 'moral defectives'. Drug abusers and alcoholics, who were diagnosed as mentally ill, could be treated under conditions of compulsory confinement, sometimes, it must be admitted, with considerable benefit.

By the 1950s a mood of therapeutic optimism had developed, with influential psychoanalysts and liberal minded criminologists advocating psychological treatment for criminals and especially for young delinquents. The use of detention for purposes of treatment, in both health and penal systems, had not yet come under sustained attack, but times were soon to change. With the recognition of the bad effects of institutionalization, unlocked wards and greater freedom for patients became fashionable. A democratic management style with patients encouraged to talk over their problems with each other and with staff was seen to be essential for a therapeutic milieu.

Legal reform encouraged such changes. The 1959 Mental Health Act promoted the idea that psychiatric patients should be treated as far as possible on exactly the same voluntary basis as other patients.

The role of magistrates in ordering compulsory hospitalization was abolished, the necessary decisions being left to social workers and doctors, but with specialist Review Tribunals set up to which patients or their relatives could appeal if they thought detention unwarranted. The courts were empowered to make hospital orders for persons guilty of crimes who were found to be mentally ill. These effectively turned over the patient to the care of the health service, with both the treating doctor and the Review Tribunal having discretion to release at any time.

In addition to mental illness and mental subnormality, the law now recognized 'psychopathy' as a condition that might warrant compulsory hospitalization. It was defined in the statute as 'a persistent disorder or disability of mind... which results in abnormally aggressive or seriously irresponsible conduct'. Given a liberal interpretation of this phrase, it would seem that doctors could recommend compulsory hospitalization for almost any form of serious and persistent misconduct. The sole limitation was a proviso that a person should not be dealt with under the Act 'by reason only of promiscuity or other immoral conduct'.

In practice, hospital orders came to be used sparingly and detention on grounds of psychopathy, especially of patients not charged with a serious criminal offence, was quite rare. There were several reasons for this. The new liberal regimes in mental hospitals were not geared to managing uncooperative and disruptive patients, unresponsive to antipsychotic medication. Hospital staffs became less experienced in handling such cases and less willing to accept them. The courts had no power to insist on admission if doctors declined. Furthermore, the efficacy and moral justification of compulsory treatments for misbehaviour came to be challenged both in the health and penal contexts. Writers like Thomas Szasz denounced unwarranted detention on psychiatric grounds and academic criminologists pointed to the absence of evidence that rehabilitation programmes for criminals had any positive effect. The badly behaved should be punished in proportion to the seriousness of their offences, not detained indefinitely on the spurious grounds that they were being cured. Such arguments helped bolster the attitude of those clinicians who regarded personality disorder, substance abuse and sexual deviation as social problems unamendable to a medical approach.

Given this background, a diagnosis of psychopathy was more likely to keep a prospective patient out of hospital than to facilitate admission. The occasional exceptions were aggressive homicidal or sexual offenders who, while not manifestly psychotic, were sufficiently abnormal for their legal counsel to seek medical evidence in support of a diagnosis of psychopathy.

Some of these were admitted via the courts by the three Special (high security) Hospitals, formally known as criminal lunatic asylums, which are meant to accommodate dangerous psychiatric patients. Even in the Special

Hospitals, however, the number of psychopaths accepted for treatment has been declining. Special Hospital patients are often given Restriction Orders preventing discharge without reference to the Home Office. Psychopaths who prove untreatable and present a continuing danger, tend to remain in hospital indefinitely, sometimes for much longer periods than they would have spent in prison had they been sentenced without reference to mental disorder. Inability to discharge the untreatable makes the doctors feel like jailors.

The 1983 Mental Health Act has added a condition that restricts compulsory detention for hospital treatment on grounds of psychopathy to cases where 'such treatment is likely to alleviate or prevent a deterioration'. This gives statutory recognition to psychiatric doubts about the appropriateness of a medical approach in these cases and provides further justification for refusing a hospital placement.

Other social and political changes have served to limit still further provisions for personality disorders. The English mental health system now emphasizes treatment in the community rather than in hospitals. Local social services have been made the lead agencies for the provision of care for persons who would formerly have been in hospital. Unfortunately, the finances of most social services are badly strained, which limits what they can provide. Allegations of neglect of the mentally disordered by the community services, resulting in preventable suicides and violent assaults, have received great media coverage, encouraged by a number of public inquiries, such as that into the case of Christopher Clunis, a schizophrenic who killed an innocent bystander.

The closure of many of the large mental hospitals has drastically reduced the number of beds for in-patients. Remaining wards are often filled to over-flowing and largely restricted to acute psychotic illness. In any event, personality disordered patients and psychotic patients need different environments and cause problems if mixed together. As in-patient places have decreased, there has been no proportionate increase in out-patient facilities or sheltered accommodation and social support for those with severe personality problems. One of the few facilities specializing in a therapeutic community approach to the treatment of personality disorders, the Henderson Hospital, was for some time threatened with closure due to funding problems. The Portman Clinic in London, an out-patient facility providing psychotherapy for social and sexual problems, is almost unique. Notwithstanding these and other outstanding examples of therapeutic endeavour, they are drops in the ocean of need. In England provision for treatment of personality disorders is woefully inadequate. There are no counterparts to the Dutch TBS clinics specializing in personality disorders.

Not all psychiatrists have pessimistic views about treating personality disorder. John Gunn, Professor of Forensic Psychiatry in London criticizes the assumption of incurability, especially when it is used to try to justify medical neglect. The great and prolonged suffering caused by personality disorders deserves attention. The incurability argument would never be used in relation to physical invalids. In one respect patients labelled schizophrenic are lucky. Although the after effects of acute phases of their illness often amount to severe personality disorder, they are more likely to be provided with the long term care that other personality disorders need, but do not receive.

The Government has shown an interest recently in reducing the number of mentally disordered individuals, who gravitate to prison. Professor Gunn's surveys have revealed a significant number of serious personality disordered individuals in the prison population. A Committee set up jointly by the Home Office and the Department of Health, under the chairmanship of Dr. John Reed, have published lengthy reports and numerous recommendations for improving service provisions for mentally disordered offenders. This Committee set up a Working Group on psychopathic disorders. Their report, long delayed in publication, made no proposals for a radical restructuring of the system or a substantial diversion of resources towards personality disorders.

The Group commissioned a review by Dolan and Coid (1993) of treatment and research issues, concerning psychopathic and anti-social personality disorders and this has been published by the Royal College of Psychiatrists. For anyone wanting to see an expansion of service, the Dolan and Coid review gave little encouragement.

The authors conclude (p.265), after analyzing some eighty studies, that 'there is no convincing evidence that psychopaths can or cannot be successfully treated'. They argue that evaluative research has so far been lacking in quality and quantity. Methodology has been defective, for example in loose definitions of the conditions included and of the treatments used, lack of adequate control groups, insufficient follow-up and conclusions drawn from small numbers of selected cases.

Despite this conclusion, Dolan and Coid emphasize that lack of proof does not necessarily mean lack of effectiveness. Scientific certainty in this field is extremely difficult to attain. They suggest that the logistical, ethical and funding problems of conducting rigorous scientific evaluations, such as random allocation to specific treatments, are at present overwhelming. They favour, in the first instance, naturalistic clinical studies informed by more detailed accounts of the patients included. They advocate careful specification of the treatments applied and the settings in which they take place as well as diagnostic evaluations of three elements: first personality disorder (making use of standardized diagnostic systems such as Hare's Psychopathy Check List); second, associated psychiatric disorders (such as mental illness, paraphiliac, addictions), and third, behavioural disturbance (such as crime, anti-social aggression or unemployability). At a later stage, when observation points to what works for what sorts of problem, definitive scientific evaluations could begin.

The authors do not want the difficulties they highlight to be used to negate the development of treatment schemes. They deprecate (p.266) the collapse of rehabilitative efforts in penal settings when criminologists found that efficacy had not been demonstrated conclusively.

Better evaluations have since shown the conclusion that nothing works in penal settings to have been premature and the same may prove to be true for treatments of psychopaths in mental health settings They point out that unsubstantiated assumptions of untreatability can be self-fulfilling and serve to discourage funding of new research. They make two more important points. Intervention should be attempted in the early stages of personality disorders, before they become hopelessly chronic, and the significant part played by social circumstances needs to be taken into account.

At the time of going to press the Government is currently considering legislation to enable mentally disordered offenders to receive a 'hospital direction' attached to a term of imprisonment. This would mean starting treatment in hospital, but finishing up in prison if discharged from hospital before the end of the sentence. Originally, the proposal was meant solely for psychopaths. It appears in line with the more punitive approach to serious offenders which has become fashionable, but it does nothing to encourage a flexible approach to treatment and rehabilitation for psychopaths.

It does appear that both clinicians and researchers have given insufficient attention to problems of personality disorder. It is some indication of continuing uncertainty that both the American Psychiatric Association and the World Health Organisation have felt the need to change their classificatory systems. Where attitude and behaviour are the presenting problems rather than medical symptoms, the expertise of clinical psychologists is often more relevant than that of other disciplines. This may account for the reluctance of some psychiatrists to become involved, but mental health treatment in England is now, at least in theory, a matter of team work. The very mixed up group of patients diagnosed as psychopathic or anti-social personality disorders, displaying as they do a multiplicity of social, psychiatric and psychological disturbances, are ideal candidates for the multidisciplinary approach.

10

Challenges as Options

Hjalmar van Marle

THE CHALLENGE FOR TREATING FORENSIC PATIENTS

The remark that fear of a custodial sentence may lead to a higher motivation for psychotherapy is important to work in the field of forensic psychotherapy. Such a 'threat' should be of course imbedded in legal and legitimate procedures and due process, in such a way that former traumata of affective neglect and parental abuse are not stirred up by impersonal or aggressive actions from the criminal justice system.

One could say that the forensic patient with his acting out seduces society to take care of him by holding him in a penitentiary setting (Van Marle 1993). Acting out for these persons often means the abreaction of inner tensions by enactment on their environment. An important cue here is to further the possibility that the patient will build up transference reactions to the treatment institution (Beyaert 1982). That means that in the experiential field of the patient the impersonal institutions are not impersonal, but behave like human beings, repeating or just not repeating behaviours already known to the patient (Van Marle 1995). As such the patient has already made his decision: he compares the treatment institution in which he is detained with his former experiences of parental figures, and from that moment the institution is immediately compared and labelled as good or bad. The affects arising from this will shape his attitude and transferences from them.

With personality disordered patients motivation for change is derived not so much from a working alliance familiar from our experiences with neurotic patients, but from their narcissistic need to incorporate us as a part of themselves. They want something from us. More than this, though, we cannot ask for from these patients.

It is up to the forensic psychotherapist to introduce gradually the principles of reality in the relationship, like a parent in the early mother–child interactions. The therapist, the group and also the forensic institution acts as an auxiliary ego, but – which is essential – they have to make themselves wanted. They can succeed in achieving this position by bringing up and clarifying those aspects of reality the patient himself fails to see because of his transference distortions. The patient can regain some of his autonomy by being able to meet other people on a mutual basis and to exchange some of his experiences with the setting.

Relying on sufficient and positive conditions of the forensic setting, the holding environment as it once should have been in a normal mother–child relationship (Winnicott 1979) is recreated with all its organizing qualities. Then it is able to form a firm base of constancy and holding, giving the patient the opportunity to lean on and to uncover his hidden motives because he needs not fear retaliation.

THE CHALLENGE FOR FORENSIC ASSESSMENT

Against this background it is possible to see more in the offence than just the act. The perpetrator reveals his unconscious self by his act and by the way he relives it in his therapy in a more or less symbolic way. As such it is possible to see in the criminal act the interactional needs of the disordered personality, the wish to be held and contained, and to be stopped from further impotence and rage. This has tremendous implications for the prison system, where not enough supportive structure in the daily program or a too harsh regime both lead to increased disorganization and acting out. With respect to their rights as detainees, forensic patients should have the possibility to earn something when they want to show responsibility, and to gain when they choose to make a relationship with some person or institution.

In fact with personality disordered patients the offence, how violent or sadistic it might be, shows the decompensation of the personality as a whole. Because of certain provocative circumstances which worked as a key in a keyhole, or because of an inner urge forthcoming from some narcissistic injury, the ego with its defence mechanisms is not able any more to contain the destructive impulses.

Society has to take over. The tension as perceived by the person as a result of this decompensation leads him sometimes to seek help, though it increases also the delinquent acting out. But still he cannot see his actions as motivated by an impending narcissistic depression.

When he perceives a kind of compulsiveness in his acts, then it is certainly a good sign for treatment. For the prognosis of our treatment it is an important distinction if the act is experienced as ego-syntonic or as ego-dystonic. In the former situation one mostly wants to blame the other for his shortcomings; in the latter one is able to blame oneself and take adequate steps for treatment. With the therapist continuously bringing reality to the fore within the therapeutic relationship, the patient is finally able to see his own contribution to the offence related situation.

To summarize so far: treatability depends not only on the personality characteristics of the forensic patient but also on the different motivational aspects of the treatment settings, where there should be opportunities for a transference relationship with the institution, including the implementation of motivational techniques (Van Marle 1991). Then contact is established.

A formal diagnosis as indication for treatment is not sufficient to acknowledge the possibilities for positive change in personality. The assessment of ego-strength is also essential as it gives clinical parameters for how much a supportive stance has to be taken in the first and perhaps later phases in the psychotherapy. Ego-strength, though primarily a psychoanalytic concept, has good clinical criteria which can be assessed easily by both ward personnel and psychotherapist, so the patient's behaviour can be distinguished between his functioning inside and outside the psychotherapy. These criteria originally put forward by Kernberg (1971) are: impulse control, anxiety tolerance, tolerance of frustrations, being able to distinguish one's own feelings from those of others and the possibility of sublimation in activities.

These positive opportunities divided from forensic assessment to achieve a relationship with the patient impinge not only on consequences for forensic treatment of mentally ill offenders, but also for the prison system as a whole. The therapeutic concept of 'holding' (Kernberg 1984) is within reach of the prison setting by introducing motivational factors on a explicit and an implicit basis to further social learning. This containment which furthers motivation for treatment can be arranged by differentiation of the prison setting, and by teaching attitudes and techniques of limit setting to the ward personnel.

THE CHALLENGE FOR A FORENSIC NETWORK

Education and training of the personnel is the concern of all the staff, not just of forensic psychotherapists. Our experience with the treatment of forensic patients has brought a lot of insight, attitudes and assessment criteria to the fore, all of which can be taught to the other workers in the field. A good momentum for this is how to cope with the rehabilitation of these patients. Rehabilitation means a shift for both patient and workers of the emphasis from intrapersonal interventions to interpersonal attitudes and expectancies. A more interactional field should be explored then with interactions that are not so well tuned as in a psychotherapy session or on a treatment ward, but having a determined behavioural and social effect.

As the number of new forensic patients increases on the waiting list, there should also be an increasing continuity with the Mental Health System. Forensic therapists have to learn that what they do will, in one way or another, have an impact on the Mental Health provisions, not only derived from their concrete work with difficult patients but also from the expectations they create with their colleagues in the MHS. While their work is only perceived as difficult and irreproducable, they will be isolated from society, just as their patients are. If this is allowed to happen, their function will be of that of guard sorcerers to bewitch the outcasts of that society, and so they become totally (and guaranteed) harmless as their profession and skills are not taken serious any more by public policy or healthcare. Instead of building an ivory tower, forensic experts should take a piece of their already fully spent time to develop strategies and lines for consultation with their colleagues outside the forensic field.

This exchange will further better indications for the services, prevent the likelihood of deteriorating psychotic patients offending and provide better care for the patients as a whole.

The challenge of a collaboration with the Mental Health System is not only restricted to the exchange of services and knowledge. Forensic psychotherapy can also be an integrated part of the advanced training programmes for residents, psychotherapists, psychologists and so forth. There is even the possibility for intervision groups with colleagues from different backgrounds, not in a therapeutic sense but from an organizational perspective. Comparison and integration of the professional and legislative standards of the different fields is needed for the continuity of care for the patients, and also for professional integrity concerning the use of medication, seclusion and involuntary treatment.

The administration, for its part, can organize projects, to be carefully evaluated, for special residential groups of forensic patients. Different outside experts can cooperate in these different treatment programmes, depending on their special skills and the nature of the project. For instance one can think about special treatment programmes for paedophiles, incest offenders, or those who have committed aggressive acts against other people. They should be enough forensic therapists because a good outcome from forensic treatment depends largely on a short waiting list. The administration can also engage in the education of young forensic therapists and psychiatrists and, of course, should be paying these employees well.

More attention should be paid to the dissemination of information about what is happening in the forensic field by assembling our experience and practical achievements and presenting it to others, as public opinion about forensic services is crucial for its development.

PART THREE

Psychotherapy and the Criminal Justice System

11

Psychopathic Disorder
and Therapeutic Jurisprudence

Nigel Eastman

Psychopathic personality disorder goes to the heart of forensic psychiatry. It is the 'junctional' case between the so called 'mad' and 'bad', and between those who clearly warrant treatment and those who should properly receive punishment. It also lies at the heart of both our ambivalence towards mentally disordered offenders as a whole and our uncertainty over whether to perceive their offending as wholly caused and explained by their disorder, or as merely expressed through the detail of their disorder. Psychopathic disorder also lies at the heart of our therapeutic ambivalence to mentally disordered offenders. Hence, it has been effectively used as an alibi to avoid offering treatment even to the frankly mentally ill, or to those who are both ill and disordered of personality (Coid 1988a). As such it often operates as the diagnostic rubbish dump of leftovers after, having applied a crude snapshot phenomenological diagnostic approach, we have determined that there is currently no mental illness present. Hence, since only personality disorder remains, the patient cannot be helped, so it is said.

The Criminal Justice System is also inherently ambivalent about psychopaths. In the criminal courts some highly disordered individuals are determined 'sane', perhaps because of a wish to punish horrendous acts, or alternatively they are perceived as highly insane, perhaps because of a fear that if such acts originate from sanity then one of us could be capable of their perpetration. Once convicted, such offenders are at risk of being randomly allocated to therapeutic and penal disposals. Further, if contained within prison, they receive little or no help, with the possible exception in England of HMP

Grendon Underwood, and are released after (usually) a determinate sentence psychologically unchanged and just as likely to reoffend as when they entered prison.

If they are detained under mental health legislation in hospital, they are likely to receive only limited and certainly under-evaluated treatment and to be at risk of being the subject of effective legal preventive detention (of which more later).

Does demonstrable medical and legal ambivalence serve effectively to confirm the lack of a valid nosological status attributable to psychopathic disorder? Should we not 'listen' to our uncertainty and simply restrict psychiatric treatment to those who can be shown to exhibit episodic (albeit potentially chronic) changes in their mental state, which make them abnormal by virtue of some comparison with their own previous normality? Ultimately, should psychopathic disorder not be written out of our legislation so that we can, so to speak, settle our psychiatric and sociolegal ambivalence once and for all? That solution has been suggested. Hence, the DHSS/HO document (1986) proposed removal of 'psychopathic disorder' from the English Mental Health Act 1983. The call was met with resistance, not only from many psychiatrists, but from the Criminal Justice System. So is psychopathic disorder a problem that will not go away, because in fact it does represent a real psychiatric and social problem entirely distinct from, say, gangsterism?

Dolan and Coid (1993) have, through a massive international literature review, demonstrated recently that there is no substantial good research evidence concerning the efficacy of treatment of psychopathic personality disorders, either one way or the other. However, assuming psychopathic disorder will not go away, are current English and Welsh legal rules relating to it therapeutic (Scotland has different arrangements)? Legal instruments and rules can be therapeutic or not in terms of, first, facilitating (or not) the individual into treatment and second, assisting (or not) the process of treatment. Let me deal briefly with each stage.

As regards getting patients into treatment, undoubtedly the Mental Health Act 1983 includes an effective mechanism. Hence, Section 1 is unusual in containing a concept which appears identical between law and psychiatry. In fact it is not, of course, identical. Legal 'psychopathic disorder' is far broader than psychiatric concepts of psychopathy. Does this difference (as well as other provisions relating to detention *per se*) operate therapeutically or not?

To the extent that the legal definition of 'psychopathic disorder' allows a very broad range of psychiatric personality disorders to be a basis for admission to hospital after an offence, it is undoubtedly potentially therapeutic in its effect. However, the extreme emphasis within the legal definition upon behaviour, potentially draws it away from psychiatry and into pure criminology. Within the legal definition, 'seriously irresponsible or aggressive behaviour' is constrained diagnostically only by the requirement that such behaviour must arise from some 'disorder or disability of mind'. The Percy Commission (1957) clearly intended that subsequent legislation should adopt a psychiatric 'term of art', but the 1959 Mental Health Act, as well as the 1983 Act, defined the term and incorporated it into legislation in such a fashion as to lay it open to abuse by society in pursuit of preventive detention, this being at the expense potentially of the therapy which inclusion of psychopathic disorder in the Acts was intended to assist. Hence, although the 1959 Act unusually included within the definition of the disorder itself 'susceptibility to treatment', and although the 1983 Act requires 'treatability' to be present before detention can occur, this provision has not operated to limit detention to situations where continued detention is based solely, or even necessarily, on the possibility of continued therapy. As a result, the doctor and patient can be legally locked into a relationship which neither believes to be therapeutic.

The best example of the 'odd duo' of a doctor and a patient who are forced, against their reason or wishes, to indulge in psychotherapy together, is the so called 'ghost train' case. Hence, a 'conditionally discharged' patient is reconvicted of a new offence, is deemed untreatable and receives a determinate prison sentence. He or she is then recalled to hospital by the Home Office just before the end of the new sentence, to be treated by a doctor who said at his or her more recent trial that he or she was untreatable. The recent decision in re A at first instance in the Divisional Court offered resolution of this psychotherapeutic and logical absurdity by determining that a patient who was detained under 'psychopathic disorder' and who was not treatable, could not continue to be detained. However, this ruling has been effectively overturned by the Appeal Court (1994), essentially by substituting 'appropriateness' of detention for medical treatment for 'treatability' *per se*. It is possible that the case could, like a number of other important mental health civil rights cases, go ultimately to the European Court of Human Rights, where one might predict a different and more 'therapeutic' legal decision.

Let me turn more clearly now to whether legal provisions assist the process of therapy, rather than merely entry into therapy. I have already assumed, perhaps not unreasonably, that legally enforced treatment where neither doctor nor patient believes it is beneficial, is highly unlikely to be therapeutic. What if only the patient adopts this position? Can enforced treatment be therapeutic? Generally, we are not concerned about the validity of non consensual treatment for mental illness, because it largely involves drugs. Is psychotherapy, of whatever form, different?

Let me state at the outset that I am not a trained psychotherapist and so I tread with some caution. However, I believe it is received psychotherapeutic wisdom that, as a general rule, psychotherapy requires a wish to change on the part of the patient and a willingness to engage in treatment. Does this render untreatable the patient who must, for Criminal Justice System reasons, be detained? Are all prisoners in HMP Grendon Underwood inherently untreatable by virtue of their detention *per se*? Similarly, is someone detained under the Mental Health Act for treatment of their psychopathic disorder not thereby treatable, because they are detained? Alternatively, must they accept the personal necessity of their own detention? These questions clearly go to the heart of important forensic psychotherapeutic issues.

First, if we refute a crude, snap shot phenomenological approach to psychiatry, then we will treat all patients, whether mentally ill or solely personality disordered, more holistically and we will reject the possibility of crudely distinguishing episodes of illness, or other behavioural disturbance, from the person in whom they occur. Hence, even the Oxford Text Book of Psychiatry (1989), bastion of phenomenological psychiatry, says: 'personality prepares the ground for illness... and determines how someone will react when ill'. The former element, personality predisposing to illness, is clearly of enormous importance in the context of psychopathic disorder, where so many patients operate on the 'border' between strict sanity and madness. Psychotic relapse may be avoided partially by prophylactic medication, but, where the origins of psychosis lie so clearly in a primarily disordered personality, there must be a responsibility on medical science at least to address the underlying cause therapeutically.

Second, it may be argued that some personality disorders, by their very nature, require 'containment' before any effective therapeutic work can be achieved. Such containment can include detention under mental health legislation, even in a highly secure environment. Incidentally, containment may even include being charged and convicted of offences which the patient has committed.

Third, if there is an imperative to attempt to treat an undoubted disorder, then, if that treatment requires detention as a necessary social or therapeutic basis, such detention cannot abolish the imperative *per se*.

Finally is there any evidence that legal detention is inherently anti-therapeutic? The Henderson Hospital, a major English example of a therapeutic community approach to treatment of psychopathic disorder, requires the lack of legal constraint. Indeed the essence of the therapeutic community model as developed at Henderson Hospital is not only individual freedom, but the sovereignty of the community itself. Is this a *necessary* part of the model? Rapport (1960) argued that the therapeutic community model is based upon 'permission to act on feelings without constraint, sharing feelings and responsibility, group decision making and confrontation'. Clearly, some of these elements are inconsistent with a regime where there are legal constraints on patients, not only in terms of their behaviour within the community, but also in terms of the requirement to remain in the community. But are these elements necessarily so therapeutically sacrosanct that any legal constraint is inconsistent with the 'best bet' psychotherapeutic model we have for treatment of serious offenders with personality disorders?

By contrast with Whitely, Norton and others who have reported on the Henderson Hospital, Craft (1965) adopted a more authoritarian regime and indeed the model at Herstedvester (Stürup 1968) is, again, different from Henderson Hospital.

I want to take the possible problems which legal compulsion may cause for psychotherapy and use them to draw us back not to question the fact of legal provisions for the treatment of psychopathic disorder, but to address the nature of those provisions. Like Coid (1993) and Chiswick (1993), I believe the current legal arrangements are misconceived, for a number of reasons, but including a therapeutic reason. Hence, justice is not served where there is potentially arbitrary allocation of offenders to prison or hospital coupled with both indeterminate periods of detention and with the legal potential for effective preventive detention.

I stated earlier that it is not only psychiatry which is ambivalent about psychopathic disorder, it is the Criminal Justice System also. I believe that such Criminal Justice System ambivalence arises from uncertainty over whether it is making and maintaining orders to offer necessary and morally justified treatment to perpetrators or to protect society from mentally disordered recidivism. Psychiatric ambivalence is nosologically inherent and unamendable to immediate change. Society's ambivalence can be settled by separating the tariff of detention from the place and purpose of detention. Hence, any law reform which allowed the setting of a tariff separately from determining whether that tariff should be served in prison or hospital, could, in my view, only be therapeutic, particularly where it has been determined that it is lawful to detain clinically untreatable psychopaths. Coid (1993) and Chiswick (1993) suggest a 'hybrid hospital order'. Others have suggested transfer to hospital from prison during the serving of a prison sentence. These appear to offer similar solutions. Essentially they do. However, there is a crucial distinction which is that one solution vests the power to place the offender in hospital with the judiciary and the other with the executive. Constitutional propriety would, in my view, point strongly towards the former. Practical politics and resource availability may argue in favour of the latter.

Let me end on two separate points, one highly specific to the topic and one of more general relevance.

Whatever legal provisions we may have in the future relating to psychopathic disorder, they must be determined not solely by the need for societal protection but also by the right of the perpetrator to justice, as well as by his or her right to treatment (or not) as addressed by the therapist and the patient. There is no place, either in terms of human rights or in terms of clinical psychiatry, for preventive detention. There is a place only for what I would term 'therapeutic detention'.

Finally, the future of psychopathic disorder is intrinsically connected with the future of forensic psychotherapy itself. For two decades British forensic psychiatry has, as it has grown in stature as a speciality, over emphasized adherence solely to the medical model. This is inconsistent with the very nature of forensic psychopathology, which even in the frankly mentally ill very frequently includes severe abnormalities of personality which are essentially unamendable to drug treatment. Recently some steps have been taken to develop forensic psychotherapy in the United Kingdom within a much wider range of mainstream forensic psychiatric services, to some extent involving my own academic department and Broadmoor Hospital. I believe these steps will operate towards ending the minority status and relative isolation from main-stream United Kingdom forensic psychiatry of forensic psychotherapy, so as to ensure a pattern of psychiatric services for mentally disordered offenders which properly arises out of the nature of their psychopathology and not out of adherence to a narrow, 'partial' model of their offending and of their treatment needs.

I was asked to offer some thoughts on whether the therapeutic implications of legal provisions for those suffering from psychopathic disorder warrant psychotherapeutic intervention and, as a result, whether legal provisions relating to some important aspects of their care are properly the subject of similar discussion. Personality abnormality is common amongst many forensic patients. Legal provisions may, to some extent, properly vary according to the extent to which such abnormality dominates or is the sole clinical problem. Hence, legal provisions may properly vary somewhat between classes of patients. However, consideration of the therapeutic effect of legal rules is a proper subject of general consideration. 'Therapeutic jurisprudence' is a highly neglected subject.

I welcome the opportunity to place it firmly on the agenda.

12

Between Couch and Bench

An Outline of Some Beneficial Effects of the Dutch Legal System on Forensic Psychotherapy

Wilma van den Berg

In conversations with therapists, in my experience they usually suppose a legal context to hamper a psychotherapeutic treatment. My proposition is that psychotherapeutic treatment of offenders can also benefit from this legal structure. In this chapter I will discuss some arguments in support of this proposition. In doing so, I will take a look at the legal system I am most familiar with, Dutch criminal law, and I will draw on my experiences as a legal counsel in the Pieter Baan Centre (PBC).

The Dutch legal system is, contrary to the Anglo-Saxon adversarial system, more (although not fully) inquisitorial. The task of the judge is not so much to examine or evaluate the material that the parties have submitted, as to find out the truth. Our penal system is also influenced by the so-called modern school of criminal law, whence came the idea that it should be possible to treat some offenders within the penal system, if that was necessary for a safe society.

According to Dutch criminal law, the court can sentence offenders to be treated by means of different modalities. If for instance a person is deemed to have diminished responsible for a serious crime and if it's likely, based on the pervasive and chronic effects of the mental disorder, that he will commit another serious crime, the judge can impose a so-called TBS, a form of coercive treatment. This is a measure of indefinite duration, which is executed in one of seven specialized, safeguarded clinics. Every one or two years the court must decide if the person's potential for dangerousness to others is still existing to such an extent that he is to be considered too great a risk to live in society, and that coercive treatment is necessary.

If someone has committed a crime under the influence of such a disturbed mental state that he is judged unanswerable for his actions, the judge has a choice: he can impose a TBS measure or he can pass a sentence of treatment in a regular mental hospital for one year. After one year the civil court can extend this period, if further coercive treatment is deemed necessary.

In case of both these coercive measures, the patient cannot of his own accord decide to discontinue treatment or to leave the clinic any more than the people who treat him can discharge him from the clinic without intervention from the court. So, at the beginning of the therapy the patient doesn't know when he will be allowed to return in the community. This can act as an incentive to both therapist and patient. If the patient doesn't cooperate, the court will generally assume that he is still dangerous, and decide that the measure of T.B.S. will be prolonged.

In some cases, this will increase the motivation of patients. On the whole, one must accept that the mentally disordered persons on whom a TBS measure is imposed, are characterized by a certain lack of motivation. They are mostly seriously mentally ill and moderate expectations as to their capacity for motivation are in order. It is on the other hand an important task for the therapists to keep on trying to motivate the patients and to explore new possibilities for treatment.

If someone is suffering from a mental disorder but the crime is not so serious, and the risk of a relapse is considered to be acceptable, then the judge can give a suspended, conditional sentence, the condition being that person must cooperate with treatment. This treatment can include out patient therapy or in patient therapy in a specific clinic, e.g. one especially suited for the treatment of adolescents or drug addicts.

The suspended sentence can be imprisonment for up to one year with a maximum probationary period of three years. If the person does not adhere to the conditions imposed on him, and if he leaves the clinic or doesn't keep his appointments with his therapist, this prison sentence can be executed.

In this modality and in the case of TBS the offender is treated within a legal context, to which in my opinion important advantages are attached.

First of all, it provides therapy with a structural framework, in the sense that the reason for and the purpose of therapy are clear and relatively well defined. The reason for the therapy is the crime the patient has committed as a result of his mental illness and its purpose is to reduce the patient's dangerousness for others until an acceptable level is attained. These aims are less clear-cut, I understand, in non-forensic psychotherapy.

The forensic therapist is also forced to define the danger that results from the patient's disorder in concrete, specific and understandable terms, and to explain why this danger has or has not decreased. For the court will examine the therapists' report and his findings critically. This impartial institution, the court, will put the results of the therapy, as reported by the therapist, to the test.

This too is an advantage of therapy in a legal frame-work. Not only does it require the therapist to focus and structure the therapeutic process for themselves – and maybe more so than they would otherwise be inclined to do – but also the presence of an independent and deciding third party of non-mental health professionals constitute a safeguard against certain therapeutic pitfalls.

There exists a tendency among therapists working in forensic settings to find a patient 'untreatable'. Interventions by the court can help to push the therapist or treatment team towards adopting a more eclectic and less restricting therapeutic style, and towards exploring new avenues of therapeutic intervention.

Another pitfall is the tendency among therapists to continue treatment beyond what is necessary, in this case beyond what is needed for a patient to deal with his problems in a non-aggressive fashion. The legal context helps the therapist to remember that 'curing' a forensic patient is not the goal, but that mitigating his dangerousness is.

In this way, the legal framework can act as a safeguard against abuse of power. It can also provide the patients with a more realistic approach to problems than the traditional medical view of the doctor who knows best and who decides all.

Every citizen has fundamental rights and in everyday life one is regularly involved in conflicts of interest, so it can be beneficial to patients to learn how to handle their rights. This also makes a clinic more like an image of society and less of an artificial environment, so the way a patient behaves in the clinic becomes a better touchstone to decide if he can be trusted to cope with living outside the clinic. Patients' rights can be important in this way.

In the Dutch criminal law system, the Pieter Baan Centrum (PBC), the forensic psychiatric observation and assessment clinic of the Dutch prison system, figures prominently. Every year 200 of the most serious delinquents are assessed in the PBC, which also advises about the indications for treatment. This clinic recommends the court from an independent point of view concerning a special group of suspects to choose between treatment within a legal framework or punishment. It concerns persons who are accused of the most serious violent or sexual crimes, whose behaviour or *modus operandi* arouse questions concerning their state of mind.

This clinic is unique for a number of reasons. It maintains an independent position within the judicial context because it is not controlled by or paid by the public prosecutor or the defence. Here the difference from the Anglo-Saxon adversarial system is striking; in that system expert witnesses always belong to one of the interested parties. In the Netherlands the impartial judge instructs the PBC to assess a suspect.

The court asks in detail about the state of mind of the accused, and about the possible connection between this mental state and the crime with which he is charged. The legal questions to be answered by the experts is: Is a mental disorder or a deficient development of the mental faculties present; was this disorder or deficiency present at the time of the crime; and if so, what is the relationship – if any – between the disorder or deficiency and the crime. The judge doesn't have to draw a sharp line between offenders who are responsible and must be sent to prison, and those who are not responsible and must be sent to a mental hospital, because of the doctrine of the diminished responsibility.

To determine the level of criminal responsibility, the Pieter Baan Centre uses a sliding scale. Five levels of responsibility are distinguished: irresponsible, severely diminished responsibility, diminished responsibility, slightly diminished responsibility and responsible. These conclusions lead to certain recommendations.

The examining magistrate – and later the court – wants to know exactly how strong the relationship between a mental disorder and the crime is and subsequently, to what extent the suspect had the freedom to act differently. How likely is it that the suspect will commit another serious crime? What can be done to prevent this? Should compulsory treatment be imposed?

If it was only this set of very special circumstances (the interaction with the victim, the long relationship and everything that had happened in the marriage) which made the suspect commit this crime, the PBC will conclude that such a person is not likely to commit another serious crime, and then there's no need for a TBS. In such cases a compulsory treatment would not serve a logical purpose.

If the PBC recommends treatment to the judge, it is usually in the shape of a TBS. This measure can only be applied if a suspect suffered from a serious mental disorder at the time of the crime. This disorder must have significantly diminished his freedom to act differently. Furthermore, if a TBS is to be considered the crime must be of a sufficiently serious nature, and the person must be dangerous for other people; it must be thought likely that he will commit another serious crime in the not too distant future.

Neither the public prosecutor nor the defence can pressure the PBC to present a more 'normal' or a more mentally disturbed picture of the accused. This makes the PBC assessment especially valuable and useful, for the court as well as for future therapists.

The PBC report is that of an expert witness and aims for impartiality. The members of the PBC team do not take sides and will refrain from writing anything that may help the judge to convict someone, or help the attorney to avoid a conviction. Information about this independent position is given to the suspects, because it is essential that they understand the role of the PBC in the legal proceedings.

The psychiatrist is not the person's doctor, who is on the 'side' of the defence. It is stated specifically to the suspects that the members of the PBC team are employed by the Ministry of Justice and that they report to the court. That means there's no room for privileged information and everything the suspects tell the members of the PBC team may be used in the report.

This striving for impartiality is especially important in cases of suspects who proclaim their innocence. Sometimes they hope that our report will prove their innocence because they hope it will show that they are mentally not capable of committing the crimes of which they are accused. In those cases, of course, the members of the team cannot discuss the crime or its possible motives with the suspect, which hampers the assessment considerably. Therefore in such cases it is sometimes only possible to describe the personality of the suspect. Neither a conclusion about the relationship between a disorder and the crime can be drawn, nor can a recommendation be made. The only exception occurs when the person suffers from a disorder that is so debilitating – like schizo-phrenia or feeblemindedness – that it affects every aspect of someone's functioning.

Other unique aspects of the PBC concern the multidisciplinary approach and the comparatively long observation period (seven weeks) on the wards. This gives us much better – and more – opportunities to try to understand and explain a suspect's behaviour, which is why usually the more complicated or bizarre cases are sent to the PBC.

For every person who is to be evaluated, a team is formed. Every team has five members: a social worker, a sociotherapist, a psychologist, a psychiatrist and a jurist. The suspect stays for seven weeks on one of our four small wards. Every ward can accommodate eight people at most. Every day the sociothera-pist keeps a record of the behaviour and attitude of the suspect, thus providing the team with relevant information, for instance about the way he interacts with the other group members. The social worker focuses on the life-history of the suspect, seen against the background of his social environment. He will try to talk to parents, teachers, friends, partners, employers and any other people who might have valuable information about the suspect. This will enable the social worker to describe in detail the specific nature of the person's life-history, to see if there are any significant discrepancies between the person's own description of his life and other people's accounts and it will help the other team members to put the person's present behaviour and state of mind in perspective.

In the PBC the suspect has a large number of conversations (an average of ten) with both psychiatrist and psychologist, who evaluate the suspect using their own professional methods.

The psychologist focuses more on the development of the personality of the suspect, supporting his clinical impressions with the results of a number of psychological tests: intelligence scales, neuropsychological tests, personality questionnaires and projective tests. These tests are aimed at providing an empirical analysis of the major psychological functions and of the personality as a whole.

The psychiatrist will try to integrate the information given to him by the other team members with his own clinical findings, using his own psychiatric impressions, focusing in particular on the specific nature of the crime and – if relevant – any pathological motives. He describes how the suspect talks, thinks and feels about the crime. The disorder and the way in which it might debilitate the suspect's functioning, or distorts his perception of reality, are discussed. The suspect's personal view and interpretation of the crime, the extent to which he realizes what he has done or negates certain aspects of his own involvement, will be compared with facts from police reports, the social workers' report, and the observation data from the ward.

Just as the legal system is the framework in which forensic psychotherapy takes place, the jurist in the PBC provides the framework for the multidisciplinary evaluation process. The jurists working in the PBC always have extensive experience working in the field of criminal law, and usually have had prior careers working for the ministry of justice, the court or the bar. One can argue that the role of the jurist in the PBC is comparable to the role of the criminal court.

The jurist will cast a critical eye on the evaluation reports of the experts, and will look for discrepancies, contradictions, vagueness, and conclusions that are insufficiently explained or corroborated. Do the experts sufficiently explain why a person is dangerous and what can be done about it? It is strictly the jurist who acts as an intermediary between the PBC, the examining magistrate, the public prosecutor and members of the bar during the seven week observation-period.

First, the jurist summarizes the documents bearing on the case, so the members of the PBC team understand the type of offence the suspect is accused of and under which circumstances it took place. There may be several crimes that can eventually result in different conclusions regarding the level of responsibility, while these various crimes may each have a different connection with the mental disorder. To give an example, a homicide does not necessarily have the same kind of relationship to such a disorder as, let's say, a burglary. The jurist is also quite sensitive to possible *culpa in causa* problems. Generally, Dutch Courts do not consider somebody who has wilfully taken alcohol or drugs to be less or not culpable, while they argue that the person who chooses to take alcohol or drugs can be held responsible for the resulting changes in the person's behaviour or mental state. This argument of course does not rule out the possibility of all kinds of interconnections between a mental disorder and the use of drugs or alcohol, and this possibility will be thoroughly explored by the PBC team.

Most important, the jurist will make sure that the questions that the examining magistrate has asked about the suspect are thoroughly addressed and answered in the report. He will so to speak 'translate' these often legal questions for the mental health experts and point out all the legal pitfalls. He will also make sure that the recommendation for treatment is practical and meaningful, in the sense that it can be fit into a proper judicial context. Not only will the jurist explain the legal questions to the members of the PBC-team, he will also make sure, by supervising the final editing of the report, that the report is understandable to a non-mental health professional, that is, the judge. If technical terms cannot be avoided, they will have to be sufficiently explained as the report will play a prominent role in the legal proceedings and will be critically read in court by the judge, the public prosecutor and the barrister.

In the PBC, we strive to write a report that answers the relevant questions and states the consequences. This goal is almost always achieved, as only in about 10 per cent of the PBC reports the psychologist or psychiatrist has to appear in court as an expert witness to clarify their findings and conclusions. Furthermore, our recommendations are followed by the judges in more than 90 per cent of the cases.

I think that this is so mainly because of the multidisciplinary principle that underlies our working method. Although the collaboration and the debates between five different groups of professionals can sometimes be very complicated, I am convinced that those very debates significantly add to the quality of our reports. In these discussions, the jurists, who make sure the questions of the court are thoroughly addressed and answered, are indispensable.

The challenge for the forensic psychotherapists is in my opinion to work within the judicial context, solving mutual misunderstandings and using judicial expertise to their best advantage.

13

Personality Disorder as a Challenge to the Criminal Justice System

Tegwyn Williams

INTRODUCTION

The challenge posed by the personality disordered for the Criminal Justice System can be simply stated as 'Who or What are they?' and 'What to do with them'. The issues of restitution and punishment have to be addressed as do issues of public safety and dangerousness. The concept of personality disorder is well recognized by layman and lawyer, who are often better able to grasp the concept that someone's personality is so disturbed as to be abnormal, than they are able to accept the whole idea of mental illness. Why then do such individuals cause so many practical and theoretical problems?

When considering these issues, I keep being drawn to the story of the elephant being difficult to describe, but everyone knowing one when they meet one. What is the relevance of this story? Most people recognize a severe personality disorder when they see one. Justice is often portrayed in the United Kingdom as a blindfolded woman, and mental health professionals are in the position of explaining the elephant to someone who cannot see – and to make things worse – does not even speak the same language.

The challenges that personality disorders cause for the Criminal Justice System echo many of those problems that mental health issues in general and psychotherapy specifically pose the legal system. In Mandarin the pictogram for challenge and danger is the same as the one for opportunity. In this paper I will highlight some of those challenges that personality disordered patients pose for the Criminal Justice System, using examples that occur in everyday practice and make some suggestions how they may be seen as opportunities for the development of forensic psychotherapy.

WHO OR WHAT IS PERSONALITY DISORDER?

Some individuals by their actions are perceived by the legal system and society as a whole to be so disordered that they require dealing with in a special way either to relieve their own distress or for reasons of public safety. These individuals are so disordered, that they must be 'mad'. This leads to challenges for the Criminal Justice System in their dealings with mental health professionals trying to clarify these issues.

The legal system sees things in black and white, guilty or not guilty, the so called binary thinking. The psychotherapeutic way of viewing things is the complete opposite of that. I remember being told by an eminent professor 'Never say never or always in medicine, medicine is all about understanding shades of grey'. Personality disorders amply demonstrate this problem; psychotherapists view the legal questions related to mental disorder as simplistic, the lawyers view the psychotherapist's explanations as vague and circumstantial.

The Criminal Justice System for the most part concerns itself with behaviours, what happened, facts that can be established by the system. Why it happened in all but the simplest sense, is less important. The psychotherapist concerns himself mostly with the why, the internal world, thoughts and feelings, intangibles that are by their very nature unprovable. The behaviour is seen only as a symptom of internal conflicts, the patient's memory of what happened being more 'important' than objective 'reality'.

The fact that there are almost as many different theoretical conceptualizations of personality disorder as there are disciplines working in the field, psychiatry, psychology and sociology, let alone every different school of psychotherapy, not surprisingly causes confusion for the Criminal Justice System, especially an adversarial one such as in the United Kingdom. If one expert can be found to say one thing, another can be found to say the opposite. Leaving aside that these differences cause interprofessional conflicts and tensions, they also undermine the validity of the whole concept.

TREATABILITY DISCUSSION

Even if the concept is valid, so what, if this does not lead to appropriate, useful advice or intervention? In other words does responsibility for such individuals really fall within the remit of the mental health services or should they, whatever the disorder, be dealt with purely by the Criminal Justice System? For example in the case of the dangerous individual, should what could be seen as preventive detention be required, should this be dealt with as purely a legal matter rather than mental health services allowing themselves to be used as a means of social control?

This leads straight to the heart of the treatability debate: are personality disorders treatable? What is treatment? In England and Wales the patient detained as suffering from 'psychopathic disorder' may only be detained in hospital for treatment, if such treatment can be shown to 'alleviate or prevent a deterioration' in the condition. However, once detained in hospital, the Mental Health Review Tribunal is not required to discharge a patient who is suffering from psychopathic disorder, simply because he is untreatable in any practical sense. This relates specifically to psychotherapy. In a recent legal ruling that involved a woman, detained with psychopathic disorder, the divisional court ruled that she did not satisfy the 'treatability test', because she refused to take part in group therapy. The Court of Appeal disagreed, making it clear that a patient is not 'untreatable', purely because they refuse the offered treatment stating 'The tribunal would no doubt have regarded to the patient's current attitude of non-cooperation, but it would not be decisive if there was a prospect that in time that attitude might change'. The legal ramifications of this legislation are still being argued about through the courts. The Criminal Justice System is not interested in esoteric debates, but in argument supported by 'facts' leading to a decision.

The innate nature and self belief, which are shown by each side of the debate fuels the tensions. Each believes that it holds the moral and intellectual high ground. The same holds true for every school of psychotherapy. This degree of egocentricity would be considered pathological if it occurred in a patient. What can be done to reduce the impact of these challenges?

Some people may argue that such tensions are the psychopathology of the personality disordered individual, being manifested in the network, exhibiting for example splitting or projection. Such interpretations do not move the debate forward, however, and do nothing to provide an opportunity for growth or reduce the conflicts and address the joint aims helping the individual and preserving public safety.

In the United Kingdom, unfortunately, it is unlikely that the legal system or legislation will alter in the short term and any progress made will have to take place in the current legal framework. Accepting that fact rather than endlessly highlighting the problems of the current system, would be a starting point.

RECOMMENDATIONS

The issue of two nations divided by a common language has to be addressed. If mental health professionals cannot make the concept of personality disorders understandable and meaningful to the non-clinical audience, it will become redundant. When relating to the Criminal Justice System, forensic psychotherapy views need to be expressed in understandable clear language, not theoretical 'psychobable' the meaning of which is only understood by the initiated. Another paradox is that psychotherapy, whose aim is to understand and clarify meaning by its language, makes meanings obscure. Psychotherapeutic insights should include the description of any disorder and appropriate intervention with realistic measurable outcomes. The conflict that what a psychotherapist views as an improvement, may not be the same as what the Criminal Justice System or the society regards, as success needs resolving. I have frequently heard argued that treatment may make the patient more likely to come into conflict with the law. This may be true, but it is a difficult position to defend outside the psychotherapeutic community. Creating a group of self-fulfilled murderers should not be our aim. We have to remember the social network in which we function.

The differences between the various different schools of psychotherapeutic thought have to be addressed and if not resolved accepted as being equally valid. Any other position undermines the credibility of the whole psychotherapeutic view.

The unifying possibility of the International Association for Forensic Psychotherapy to this end should not be underestimated. Some organizations have to be seen as representing such views and feeding these into the Criminal Justice System at a policy level on national international stage.

My experience is that as individuals, members of the Criminal Justice System are open to new ideas, but as a body they view change slowly. The current political climate in the United Kingdom does not favour such education. The rehabilitation of offenders is not a priority, punishment of them is. More prisons are being built in both the public and private sectors at considerable cost, to hold the ever increasing prison population. Regimes in prison are being made more austere. Recent Home Office (the department of government that deals with internal affairs) studies which linked crime with low levels of employment, suggested that monies spent on building prisons could be better spent on job creation, but this information was not made public. Politicians are accepting advice from their officials less. A senior civil servant resigned recently, citing that public policy was often decided from a party political rather than an informed position, to the extent that current policy now actively discourages the seeking of information that may contradict the political view. The executive and the judiciary are losing faith in the elected politicians. Against such a background the concept and the challenge of personality disorders are both of great importance to the Criminal Justice System and society as a whole. To be heard, the psychotherapeutic view needs to be expressed as clearly and forcibly as possible.

Seduction of the Regime

Enda Dooley

While I am by training a forensic psychiatrist, I am not a trained psychotherapist. As a result, I am not saddled with the baggage of belief (i.e. of belonging by training to one or other particular school of psychotherapy). My present responsibilities are mainly administrative, but involve liaison with a variety of professional disciplines, both within and outside the prison system. Consequently, my contribution will be at a somewhat 'concrete', pragmatic level.

Social policy is influenced by the public who (possibly through the media) influence politicians. These, in turn, bring pressure to bear on civil service administrations who have ultimate responsibility for the provision of therapeutic services. Within the particular therapeutic field in which I am involved (treatment in a prison environment), cost also becomes a factor in service provision. Increasingly, any therapeutic services provided at state expense (including to prisoners) are influenced by the perception of 'value for money' provided. Any therapeutic process proposed, needs to be justified, not only in terms of probable or possible benefit, but also in terms of cost.

To date psychotherapeutic interventions with prisoners have been beset with problems of establishing and maintaining credibility. In this context credibility depends on making the process (including its problems) accessible to lay people – while they may not partake in the process, they understand what is happening and support the interaction. The therapeutic process (including the therapist) needs to be accessible on a practical basis, especially regarding prognostic considerations. In the prison (or other public funded situation) the concept of the therapeutic interaction occurring free from outside influences, for unlimited duration, without any accountability, no longer holds.

This gives rise to a conflict between the pragmatic need of the funder for a clear programme or schedule of therapy (which can be costed, etc.) and the open-ended, unstructured process of many dynamic therapies.

Of increasing importance in relation to various forms of dynamic therapy is the competence of the therapist. This has arisen with the explosion of various forms of 'counselling', many claiming to be therapeutic processes, undertaken by people of indefinite background and training. As someone responsible for overseeing the provision of treatment to prisoners, I feel obliged to ensure their 'right to competence'. If necessary, I consider that in certain situations no therapy is preferable to what may be undertaken by a therapist who is ill-trained for what is often complex and demanding work involving prisoners. A variety of situations, often involving incompetent therapists, has led to a perception by those managing prisons that any form of psychotherapeutic intervention with prisoners is a 'naive' process, wasteful of scarce resources. The challenge to bodies such as the International Association for Forensic Psychotherapy is to work to overcome this perception.

To come back to the title of this chapter – the challenge for social policy – I perceive the challenge as that of overcoming the social and political desire to punish. We are currently in an era of therapeutic nihilism in the prison context. This conflicts, however, with the pressure from the public that something should be done to 'cure' those who have offended society, while they are incarcerated. The epitome of this conflict is in relation to the management of sex offenders, where increasingly draconian sentences are accompanied by demands for therapeutic intervention.

To overcome the perception of psychotherapy as being a waste of time and resources, there is a need on the part of the therapist to exhibit benefit pragmatically in terms of cost, accessibility, etc. Social policy makers are unimpressed by games of academic or intellectual chess between schools of therapeutic thought. Statements that prisoners or others should have a particular course of therapy and that benefit (often unspecified) will result, are met by (at best) benign indifference.

To promote the involvement of psychotherapy in the prison environment a process of seduction is involved where the therapist makes him or herself indispensable to the regime and is perceived as performing a useful and practical role. This is likely to have much greater success than the bludgeon of insisting that a particular therapy should occur as by right without any effort to justify it in terms of practical benefit.

15

The Challenge for Planning Social Policy

Irma Ballering

The biggest challenge for planning social policy in the area of forensic psychiatry is to keep all parties concerned happy and satisfied. These parties are among others: the patients themselves, victims and their relatives, the psychiatric hospitals, public prosecutors, judges, professional groups and the Ministries of Justice and of Health, Welfare and Sport (HWS). Each group has its own expectations, tasks and responsibilities, which are by no means always in tune with each other.

The society as a whole just wants to put troublesome mentally disturbed persons away. These patients or offenders are often very reluctant to undergo treatment in any sense. The therapists on the other hand want to provide the best care and treatment for their patients in properly equipped hospitals.

Another problem the Dutch policymakers are facing is the fact that two ministries are involved in the care of forensic psychiatric patients, namely the Ministry of HWS and the Department of Justice. The first responsibility of the Department of Justice is to maintain law and order, and to execute sentences and coercive measures, whereas the prime task of the Ministry of HWS is the treatment and care of patients, whether they have committed crimes or not. The responsibility of the former ends as soon as the sentence has been served, but the responsibility of the health care system is further reaching. A patient is often already mentally disturbed before he commits a crime, and he will stay in this condition after the judicial intervention. The words: 'patient from cradle to grave', are commonly used in this sense.

Both Ministries have been faced with the following problems.

1.   Growing waiting lists for in-patient facilities.

2.   Reluctance in general mental hospitals to take in this group (which to some extent is due to the process of deinstitutionalization and to unfamiliarity with the group of forensic patients).

3.   Obstruction of the TBS hospitals.

4.   Lack of (cheaper) aftercare facilities.

5.   Financing all the required facilities.

Only in the past few years has it become clear that to tackle these problems a joint policy of the ministries is preferable. An effort is made to avoid shifting the responsibility to the other party concerned. Instead the ministries plan and coordinate together. By doing so, they attempt to achieve a careful balance between protecting the society and serving the interests of the patient, who requires treatment and who will eventually return to the society.

This joint policy contains the following intentions:

1.   Expansion of the clinical capacity.

2.   The development of specific aftercare facilities and start of a registration system.

3.   Networking in order to improve the throughput or patient flow from one system to the other.

PLANNING OF EXPANSION OF CLINICAL CAPACITY IN BOTH SYSTEMS

At this moment the Netherlands have six special TBS hospitals where patients with a TBS order are cared for. The Minister of Justice bears final responsibility for them, although 80 per cent of the costs are carried by health care through the Exceptional Medical Expenses Act. Beside these Hospitals, there are two forensic psychiatric clinics which are health care institutions. In these clinics TBS patients are admitted, alongside patients who are detained in another legal context. The concept behind this distinction is that the TBS hospitals are especially equipped to treat patients with a personality disorder, whereas forensic psychiatric hospitals have more experience with treating psychotics. Nowadays, this distinction has lost its value. The rapid increase of the number of violent psychotic patients with a TBS order compelled the Ministry of Justice to admit psychotics in TBS hospitals too.

The capacity of the existing institutions is not sufficient. That is why a seventh TBS hospital is being built as well as a third Forensic Psychiatric Clinic. However, figures have indicated that even this expansion will not be enough in the near future. In addition to these special hospitals, the Ministry of Health has appointed four mental hospitals to create special wards for forensic psychiatric patients. This was done by way of experiment. As the experiment proved to be successful, we are planning to expand the existing wards and to create several new ones.

It has become more and more obvious that not only something has to be done about the inflow of the hospitals, so there will be sufficient places for treatment, but the output of these facilities also requires attention. If we disregard the output, the result will be that no expansion ever will be enough. It has emerged that the patients transferring to facilities within the general mental health care and other social services regularly encounter difficulties. Among other things, the reasons are the stigma of having been in a custodial institution and the fact that there is no possibility of return to the Forensic Psychiatric Hospitals, if problems arise. To counter these problems a few developments in the frontier between the forensic services and the mental health system are supported. These are the following.

DEVELOPMENT OF SPECIAL AFTERCARE FACILITIES

An important and challenging objective is the development of aftercare facilities. After their release from an institution, a considerable number of patients (about 50%) will have to rely on specific aftercare facilities such as sheltered housing. A number of sheltered homes within the health care system has already admitted several forensic patients. In the next few years the capacity for special sheltered homes will increase further. The advantage of creating these facilities is twofold. On the one hand it offers the opportunity for a patient to return sooner to the society and on the other hand the costs in these facilities are much lower than in the TBS hospitals and other forensic in patient facilities.

A major role in aftercare is played by the out-patient clinics and day treatment facilities, which have been recently created by a number of TBS hospitals. With these provisions, forensic patients can be released earlier while others, not in need of detainment, can have a ambulatory forensic treatment in accordance with the latest developments.

REGISTRATION SYSTEM

The two ministries have started a pilot project in Amsterdam to register the so-called through traffic from the judicial system to the health care system. In this way they hope to find out what capacity is needed within the health care system to accommodate forensic patients in need of common psychiatric services. When it is clear that this registration system can have its monitoring and informative function, efforts will be made to implement this system nationwide and to register the specific needs for treatment. In the Meijers Institute in Utrecht a monitoring system is also developed to register the through traffic in the TBS system itself, and from the TBS hospitals to the mental health systems.

NETWORKING

In some parts of the Netherlands institutions have started a network within their region which facilitates coherent care for this special group. The ministries look upon this development as a perfect way to solve many organizational problems which emerge when two different systems have to work together. As a result they try to facilitate these networks wherever possible.

Such a network should include a TBS hospital and/or a Forensic Psychiatric Clinic, a general mental hospital, an out-patient clinic and day treatment facilities, sheltered homes, and also judicial organizations, like the after care and resettlement organization.

The main functions of a network could be:

o to increase the level of professionalism in the general mental health circuit

o guaranteed returns to former institutions

o crisis intervention

o setting up a system for indicating patients on medical and psychiatric grounds

o reaching agreements with associated care systems

o case management.

From the objectives mentioned above, all psychiatric patients will benefit. New challenges already appear on the horizon. However, there will always be groups for which the modern methods of treatment will not be appropriate. This means for instance that there will always be people who are beyond treatment and who will never be able to return to the society. Currently, it is this group that's obstructing the expensive TBS hospitals and the forensic hospitals.

The question remains as to what should be done with this category? Do they belong in the modern mental hospitals which, during the last decades, lost most of their original asylum function, or should set up special secure facilities be created within the judicial system? And should these facilities be more like a prison or like a half way house on the premises of the TBS hospital?

Another problem group is that of the forensic patients with two disorders: those mentally ill offenders who also have a serious drug abuse problem. There are far reaching plans to found a forensic addiction clinic for offenders with a drug abuse problem. Should the next step be a special clinic for double diagnosed forensic patients?

CONCLUSION

Registration, networking and the planning of special facilities for proven problem groups are therefore the main lines along which the Dutch developments occur on this moment. Experiences from the past have brought the insight that all these developments should be accompanied by thorough research.

16

Our Responsibilities as Forensic Psychotherapists

Christopher Cordess

'Personality disorders', which were until fairly recently addressed to a limited degree in the psychodynamic and psychoanalytic literature as their near relatives, 'character disorders', are indeed a challenge. At one extreme they are a challenge jointly to the legal system and to us as psychiatrists and psycho-therapists: at another they are a challenge to us all as our own versions of character disorder and neuroses. Although categorial distinctions have practical and legal currency and usefulness, it is well to remember that we exist on a dimension of human kind: 'them and us' will not do, even though it may give us a warm feeling of our own superiority as members, as it were, of 'the moral majority'.

I agree therefore that we should not define personality disorder according to biological variants although neither should we ignore them as possible correlates. Defining them according to a functional psychopathology of psychological and social dysfunctions has many advantages, not least for the forensic psychotherapist in requiring him to question and acknowledge his own psychological limitation. This approach has profound relevance for issues of our own countertransference. A major clinical difficulty in this area is how to discriminate between those offenders whom it is possible to engage therapeutically and are possibly 'treatable', and those who are not. At a personal level I experience it as: 'Can I make contact with (and possibly help) this person, could someone else, or is he (at the present time at least) unavailable for any therapeutic intervention?'

The Dutch legal and TBS system, is an exemplar of human and therapeutic optimism, which – in the particular case of personality disorders – is not shared within other jurisdictions, including the British. We are, possibly excessively, sceptical and characteristically ambivalent. A recent survey of all forensic psychiatrists working in Britain split half and half upon whether 'Psychopathic Disorder' should remain within our Mental Health Act. But a majority (90%) considered that 'a multidisciplinary approach' should be offered, against only a minority who believed that 'psychopaths are untreatable (Cope 1993). The debate hinges around whether treatment should happen by detention in hospital 'without limit of time', or whether those suffering from personality disorders should be sentenced to prison. There is, however, only one therapeutic prison – for two hundred people – in our whole system.

In the line with Cope's finding, Coid and Dolan (1993), in their recent comprehensive review of personality disorder, conclude that 'there is no convincing evidence that 'psychopaths' can or cannot be treated'. They make the point, however, that definitions have been loose, treatment ill-defined, and that the evaluation of treatments have been mostly short term and limited in scope.

As a practising forensic psychiatrist and psychotherapist, it seems to me that we cannot shrink from this, our central and crucial challenge: personality disorders in their various guises are our subject. There is increasing evidence that disorders of personality are associated with personal histories of failed attachment, neglect and frequently physical and sexual abuse. They are developmental disorders of the integrity of self, of self-awareness and of empathy for others. We have, therefore, a duty in both planning preventative – social, educational and health – policy, and of offering care and psychological understanding to at least some of these unfortunate people. But we cannot and should not expect miracles, nor offer them to our legal and political colleagues who quite correctly feel that 'something (other that merely custodial treatment) should be done', and put us under pressure to offer the impossible. Gunn and Taylor (1993), for example, have criticized the expectation of 'curability' on the grounds that such arguments would never be used in cases of physical illness. In some cases we should be aiming for support, rather than for radical change.

I believe that our task is to keep trying, but to temper whatever therapeutic zeal we have with clear definitions of our aims and with well designed evaluation of our treatment methods and outcome.

This admonition can seem hollow – as indeed, previously it has to me. However, new and exciting research methodologies in psychotherapy have become available: for example, the work beginning to be generated by the use of the *Adult Attachment Interview* (George *et al.* 1985). This research instrument is beginning to be used with populations of offender patients. It offers the possibility of assessing 'internal' (mental) representations of attachment figures, and getting at a quantitative and qualitative assessment of such personality characteristics as self-esteem and the capacity for empathy. These are essential elements in much serious offending and in the prediction of risk of violent behaviour. It also offers the possibility of measuring change over time.

PART FOUR

The Reality
of the Victim

17

The Challenge of the Victim

Gwen Adshead

INTRODUCTION

It has been my privilege (and sometimes my misfortune) to work with both victims and offenders. Sometimes, those groups were one and the same people. It has been my experience that work with traumatized or victimized people is the hardest work there is. Forensic psychotherapists do not need to be told this; they perhaps knew this before anyone else, because they saw the victim in the offender. But this chapter will suggest that work with victims is a real challenge, because it is hard work. It will discuss why such work is hard (and not getting easier), and will attempt to identify those elements of difficulty which relate to the workers, and those which relate to the victim. A discussion of how such work may be made easier will conclude the chapter.

THE CHALLENGE OF THE NUMBERS
AND THE NATURE OF VICTIMIZATION

The sheer numbers of victims is a challenge: those direct victims who are injured in war, by assault, by illness or natural disaster. There are indirect victims also: the families of victims or offenders. There are also those who might be called 'licit' victims: those who are victimized, because they offend. The focus of this paper are those who are the victims of other's brutality. Those who are victims of accidents or natural disasters might be more accurately called survivors. In this sense, although undoubtedly traumatized, one is not victimized by, say, a typhoon or the sinking of a ferry. Those who suffer at the hands of others are victims.

The implications of the words 'traumatization' and 'victimization' require exploration. Trauma implies a shattering; of links and of affective bonds, a shattering of attachment to others (De Zulueta 1993), of the capacity to think (Garland 1991). Both thinking and feeling are severely affected by trauma. Garland also emphasizes that previous neurotic defences and fantasies about childhood trauma are exposed by disasters and may not be strong enough to withstand the stress. How adults handle trauma in adulthood is profoundly affected by their earlier experiences of trauma in childhood (Bremner *et al.* 1993).

Victimization, however, involves all these features of trauma, but much more, because the source of the trauma is human. The psychiatric literature on post-traumatic stress (PTS) makes it clear that it is worse when it is caused by human agencies (Raphael 1986). Bonnie Green, in reviewing the literature, reminds us that the traumas that cause most PTS are those where human atrocities are witnessed or perpetrated (Green 1993).

Victimization implies a *connection* between the victim and the offender. The offender's concentration is focused on the victim in a way that should suggest intimacy, but is in fact the height of objectification. There is a high degree of intimacy in that the offender chooses his victim, and the victim is completely dependent on the offender; and simultaneously, there is none. Where there is a prolonged assault, there may be moments of ambivalence, tenderness even between the victim and their aggressor, but this is usually followed by even greater violence. In the moment of attack, the offender has no interest in the victim at all. There is a complete distortion of everything that we consider valuable about human relationships.

It is clear that most victimization takes place in the context of a relationship. Most murder victims are murdered by a close friend or partner. Children are most likely to be sexually and physically assaulted or killed by their parents. Women are most likely to be raped by men they know. In Bosnia the offenders and victims are neighbours. Relationships essentially involve dependence and behaviours that stimulate dependence (Bowlby 1988).

The dependence aspect of victimization is *crucial*, because early childhood experiences of dependence (whatever they were like) are likely to be replicated, especially with those who seek to help the victimized. Dependency also entails vulnerability, weakness and a requirement for protection. This in turn gives rise to fantasies and fears of abandonment, which in the moment of victimization come true. You are in trouble and no-one comes. Your distress and protest is ignored. Nothing you can do can make a difference. Being assaulted is the ultimate infant nightmare.

HELPLESSNESS AND THE VICTIM

Being helpless is a crucial factor in the victim experience. The word 'victim' has become a dirty word; 'survivors' is preferred, because it does not carry the implications of helplessness and vulnerability, which are (apparently) unacceptable. I think this is to deny the reality of the horror of being victimized. Clearly this denial happens at a number of levels and for a number of reasons, which I will discuss later. Perhaps at this stage, I will just say that we lose the use of certain words at our peril, and the word 'victim' is too important a word to be denied existence.

It is important to ask how dependence, vulnerability and helplessness have come to be seen as unacceptable, even disgusting. Although usually seen as related, there is nothing about being dependent that *necessarily* implies total helplessness. What is implied perhaps is a giving up, or sharing, of control. I become dependent on you, I now no longer have total control over a part of me identified and invested in you. I will have to rely on you to keep me in your mind and keep me safe. Dependency needs are perhaps some of the *conscious* manifestations of projection and projective identification, and are of course a normal and healthy part of social life. They are also an important part of moral life. The conscious aspects of projection and identification are the psychological basis for our duties towards one another.

The victim is truly helpless before someone in whom they have a great deal invested. Where the attacker is a stranger, the victim has a lot invested in finding out as much about him as possible without upsetting him. If the attacker is known, the victim may have a lot to lose by antagonising him. Often the attacker is someone who is loved and to whom the victim is attached, both consciously and unconsciously.

The final aspect of helplessness and victim status is that of a real power imbalance. There is very little a child can do against an adult determined to assault him. There is very little a woman can do against a man who is determined to assault her. There is little a man can do against another man who is armed, or a group of men intent on assaulting him. Aggressors select victims who are vulnerable, against whom they can win. This experience of helplessness, especially when the assaults are carried out over a long period of time, leads to both a deep despair and misery and a deep and vicious rage. The victimized person devises both conscious and unconscious, cognitive and affective strategies to separate from the traumatic experience. One of the first strategies is to despise the hurt self and disown it. For psychotherapists, working with both victims and offenders in the same person, this is the most dangerous moment. The hurt self must not be allowed to die, or be repressed; there must be pity for one's own distress, or there will be no pity for the distress of others.

SPECIALNESS: IDEALIZATION AND DISTANCE

Victims become 'special'. They have a special experience and a special knowledge that sets them apart from others. This can be both a lonely and a grandiose experience, with the grandiosity being both part of the experience and a defence against the loss and fear in the victim experience. The 'specialness' of the victim is a crucial problem in treatment. This was described best by Main (1957) and many victims need to go back to being ordinary again and to lose their specialness before they can recover. I shall discuss this further below.

There are two features of being special which deserve attention, because of the potential effects on therapy: idealization and distance. Idealization takes place through the ennobling of victim status and the association with religious rituals: 'They dressed him with garlands like a victim' (Frazer 1922). Idealization is reflected in the idea that the human victims represent gods, who are then kept alive by their image's death.

The concreteness of thinking is noteworthy; that the victim sacrificed literally turned into the thing to be feared or desired. This reflects not only a primitive level of anxiety, but also the degree of anxiety that is allayed by the victim's sacrifice.

Idealization may be hard to maintain. For example, the victim who is sacrificed for others' sins becomes identified with those sins. The word 'scapegoat' makes clear the connection between sinning and sacrifice. There is thus a fine distinction between the victim and the scapegoat, who takes on everyone's wrongs or crimes. Many offenders become victims by being scapegoats, and victims become offenders by the same mechanism.

In order to destroy a victim and maintain the idealization, cognitive and affective distancing from the victim is necessary. This takes place by two methods: physical and mental. Those who organized the sacrifices of old kept the victims separate physically from others. Concentration camps and prisons are obvious examples. In other circumstances the media may contribute to this sort of distancing. The bereaved often say that others avoid them. Victims thus feel isolated and unable to reach other and confirmed in their 'specialness'.

The mental knowledge that the victim has of violence and death makes him special and also feared. A 'special' knowledge also increases our fascination, hence the fascination of the tabloid press with victims and the constant debate about whether pictures of 'real' suffering should be portrayed in the press and on the TV. Victims themselves know that their knowledge is special, which helps to maintain the distance. Victims often say 'only someone who has been through it would understand'. This disables and deskills others and decreases the chance that others can listen and hear. It is true that others find it difficult to listen, but it can be hard for victims to believe that others want to hear and will not be destroyed by the story. The '1000 mile stare', described by the

Vietnam veterans, sees something that others do not, and fears that others dare not look and see.

It is also important here to reflect on the internal experience of specialness, which help to maintain distance. The special knowledge becomes secret, putting boundaries between those who know and those who do not. This is why incest is so destructive and why sexual abuse stops communication. There are no secrets when one is communicating. Everyone has infantile fantasies of secrets that might be held, of exclusive relationships that will never end. But this type of secret knowledge was meant to remain in fantasy and not to be made real. Therefore real knowledge of special experiences is not comfortable, and others do not want to hear it.

In philosophical terms, a victim is both harmed and *wronged.* Clearly, there are physical, psychological and spiritual harms to the victim. Bur the victim is also wronged, because they become an object for the use of others. Within the Kantian ethical discourse, doing the greatest good requires us to always treat others as ends in themselves and not merely as means to ends. Objectification is another means of distancing ourselves from victims. It is arguable that this is a *wrong* that causes most harm, that shatters self-esteem and the ability to trust, especially when the offender is one in whom all trust was placed.

There are many ways to understand these reactions to victims. Idealization is a defence against the reality of suffering and a defence against guilt that it is someone else who is suffering. If successful enough, idealization can be distorted to a kind of envy of the specialness and hatred for the victim. The distance helps to maintain the illusion that the victimization experience can never happen to oneself and that victims are a breed apart. Again, a reluctance to accept the meaninglessness of violence, and the utter objectification inherent in victimization can lead to further blaming of the victim; she wanted it to happen, she provoked it, he started it.

SUFFERING AND SADISM: BEHIND THE IDEALIZATION

Idealization of the victim has another purpose. It is a perverse defence against acknowledging the sadism of others. Behind the idealized garlands, we also find not only the denigration of the victim, but the sadism of the aggressor. This may be understood as the *denigration* of the vulnerable and the dependent, and the *pleasure* in destroying or hurting anything that is vulnerable.

I raised earlier the notion that, after cumulative trauma, the victim ceases to care about herself. She blames herself and by identifying with the aggressor, comes to despise her own suffering, which makes it easier to bear. Self-blame also offers a sense of control over suffering, and protects the aggressor both consciously and unconsciously, which is useful when one is being assaulted by someone one loves. Fairburn described this as the 'moral defence' (1952). Like most converts, the victim is likely to have more despite for suffering than even her aggressor. The expression of vulnerability or dependence in others can therefore elicit the strongest of sadistic feelings. This sadistic arousal is fuelled by anxiety; a veritable panic that long repressed pain and distress will be stimulated in response to another's distress. This cannot be allowed to occur. Brutal systematic ablation of the victim, the source of this expression and dependency, will take place. The victim becomes the victimizer.

The rage and aggression that victims can and do express, should therefore give us no surprise. However, it is uncomfortable to hear this, because it makes suffering real and allows us to see how we are using the victim for our own ends. So the sadism either needs to be completely hidden or rewritten as something noble. Something of this can be seen in the idealization of political or religious martyrdom. What is striking, however, is the tremendous reluctance to accept that victims can be angry and dangerous *because* of their victimization. Distance is driven between the victims and the aggressors, with little under-standing that where there is a victim of serious interpersonal violence, there will be a potentially dangerous person. There may be many factors that mitigate this potential, but the risk should be noted.

FROM PAST TO PRESENT: THE INTERNAL GODS

At this point the view is often expressed that understanding the offender's victim experience is an attempt to excuse all offenders. But this is illogical (and false), because excuse and understanding are phenomenologically quite differ-ent. Also those who seek to understand have a different job, in relation to the offender, than those who seek to blame; but both jobs are necessary. But it somehow seems *intolerable* to understand the aggressor in terms of victimiza-tion, and accept the reality of their suffering.

At a social level, groups of people are happy to blame the offender's victim, call them provocateurs and denigrate dependency and vulnerability; while, at an individual level, the same people call for the most severe sanctions and punishments against offenders.

There are new gods to appease and maintain, to whom victims are now sacrificed. The savage gods are all internal now; victims are sacrificed to appease internalized impotence, rage and grief. They are also sacrificed to show others how dangerous the aggressor is, and as an expression of sadism. Anthropologi-cally, the savage gods or tribal fathers represented the dangerous and unpre-dictable elements that once ruled our lives as huntergatherers or farmers. Organized religion tried to introduce control over those gods and this control leads to much cruelty and human sacrifice of various kinds. Now organized religions are seen as anachronistic, meaningless and dangerously irrational. But it is not clear that we are so much better off, now that we do not believe in savage external gods. 'There is no God', we say and 'Anyone who believes in a religion is a fool', or 'Religion does a lot of harm'; well, there are no gods and still victimization continues. We were so anxious to get rid of the external gods, we did not notice that we had internalized them.

A FURTHER CHALLENGE: LARGE GROUP RESPONSES

The dynamics of the internal world are acted out in group form in the external world, and group dynamics add another dimension to internal chaos. In Bosnia many of the 'forces' that victimize are internal, but are acted out externally and grow in the group dynamic. This phenomenon of the group altering as an expression of the mass of the individuals is well described in nature (see Fox Keller 1985).

The acting out of internal world dynamics in the form of social attitudes also contributes. As forensic professionals, in the thick of the space between victims and offenders, we need to understand these large group social responses. If distance and idealization are perverse cognitive and affective defenses erected against trauma, then groups, as well as individuals, can become perverse by using perverse cognitive structures and primitive defences: splitting, projection, idealization and denigration, intolerance of ambivalence.

In his book, *The Culture of Complaint*, Robert Hughes (1993) describes these mechanisms in relation to modern American culture. Hughes describes what he believes is a new modern mythology in which everyone is a victim and there seems to be an inability to tolerate complexity and ambiguity. Differences and disparities between groups imply total separation; unless we are all the same, we cannot understand one another. The primitive quality of this type of thinking is obvious; what Hughes does not discuss is the underlying anxiety that any victim may be an offender, and *vice versa*.

By keeping the victim and the offender separate, social groups maintain difference and allay anxiety about difference. This disempowers both victim and offender by denying the reality of their feelings in one group. Pity and sympathy are acceptable, but not rage and the danger, *vice versa* in another group. Lifton (1973) describes this in relation to Vietnam veterans coming home full of rage. A familiar cognitive polarization takes place: us and them, victims and offenders, rage and pain, presented as essentially different. 'Victims' are not seen as dangerous and offenders are not seen as in need of sympathy.

This mechanism is found within the prisons and secure hospitals in which we work. The offenders are victimized and their victim experience ignored. Any challenge to this produces anxiety and repressive actions (e.g. no time for therapy for offenders in prisons). Similarly, the victim's sense of protest and outrage against the offender may be dismissed as 'they must be biased'.

At the large group level, perverse mechanisms may be seen in the persecution of difference and the vulnerable: the repeated victimization of women by men, of children by parents, of men of colour by whites. Sinners are persecuted for carrying all the projections of fantasized sins of others; e.g. ridding the world of prostitutes is a common theme for some male serial killers. Most serial killing is very ritualistic and the victims are carefully chosen. Such persecution stands as a warning to other potential victims and keeps them in fear (Brownmiller 1975; Stanko 1990).

The reality of the victim's experience is denied. We identify with the aggressor and denigrate the victim. We write papers that talk only of the victim's masochism and nothing of the aggressor's sadism. We ask: 'Why does she stay?', not 'Why doesn't he stop?' We refuse to accept that there is wrong doing; that there are victims who do not contribute to their own victimization. Although we need to be able to tolerate affective and cognitive ambiguity, this does not mean that all situations are ambiguous. Sometimes the experience is clear, and attempts to make it seem ambiguous are defences against the reality of sadism and suffering.

Related to this is the professional rejection of our own vulnerability and the denigration of those, who admit to feeling. Affective experience in professional life may become denigrated generally, so that only 'objective' discourses are seen as valuable. Doctors are the last group to acknowledge their own needs. This may be reflected in the incidence of substance abuse and illness in doctors.

THE DISCOURSE OF THERAPY: THE CHALLENGE OF THE VICTIM

Damaged people are dangerous: they know they can survive. We need to be able to acknowledge the dangerousness. Victims may be especially dangerous towards those who claim to care for them. Bowlby (1988) noted that abused children are aggressive towards caretakers. The abused child experiences a savage combination of rage and impotence, causing massive anxiety and arousal. If this is not eased in any other way, then violence will ease it. Initially this usually takes the form of deliberate self harm. The attention this brings and a sense of being cared for, sometimes makes things worse, because it further stimulates the sense of dependency, which is so painful. For those whose sense of self was impaired before and whose self-esteem is therefore low, *any experience of self may increase rage.*

What then can psychiatry do? It may be better first to think of what it cannot do; to make everything all right again, or to make what has happened acceptable. There is no reparation for most of our patients. The chief task must be damage limitation, and there are a number of therapeutic strategies for this.

1. It is important to attempt to make the trauma containable. In Bion's sense the therapist becomes container and maker of meaning, and the therapeutic time becomes a space for the digestion of pain. One may use different means to this, such as cognitive behavioural work as well as transferential work. The therapist helps the victim to achieve ability to think: to symbolize, to have words to tell their story.

2. The therapist may have to alter technique (Freud 1919); especially in different settings (Main 1989). She may place more emphasis on support, or 'keeping people company'. Victimization leaves one very alone. Support means being there: 'being with', rather than 'doing to' (Wolff 1971). This not only means helping the patient bear as much as he is able, but also knowing one's own limits of what one can bear.

3. The therapist needs to be able to hear and tell the truth about experience, and to let various truths stand. An account of an assault will contain several truths, which all have a reality. (The best example of this is Kurosawa's film 'Rashomon'.) At the moment, the victim's truth is rarely heard. At the movies you will not experience the pain of the victim who dies or is injured, although you may experience the thrill of killing and injuring. In the courts you will hear that the dead or injured brought their suffering on themselves; you will not hear that their assailants were thrilled or excited when inflicting suffering. It is painful to face up to the challenge of letting the voices of victims speak and bear witness, as anyone who has read the works of Primo Levi will bear out. Both sides of the story must be heard without assuming an adversarial imperative to determine truth. There is no single 'truth' in the therapeutic space, or, at least, not the sort of truth that exists in a test tube or in a court of law.

4. Telling the truth may require us to be radical therapists. We may have to be political in every sense; being prepared to say that some actions or positions are not acceptable, if that is our view. Forensic psychotherapy, working with both the victim and the offender, cannot claim moral neutrality. Repeatedly hitting or biting a child is not acceptable; we need to make this clear to the adult who does this, and to both the victim in memory and the victim in reality. We can try and understand; we must do so. But we cannot imply that certain actions are acceptable, just because we understand them.

5. There are other challenges in the therapy of the victim. The splitting of different types of feeling needs to be challenged: the pain and fear of the offender, the murderous rage and viciousness of the victim. We need to face our own internal challenges to the reality of trauma; what DH Lawrence calls the 'kissing and horrid strife, the angels and

sunderers'. We need to provide supports for our own anxiety, especially when we have to challenge rigid claims of difference and polarization. We may have to contribute what we can to attempts to rediscover how to live with ambivalence and connection with difference.

We may also have to challenge the professional *status quo*; what Lifton described as 'revolutionary psychiatry' in which we reclaim the life of the feeling and develop our services to help the victims survive. Our aim may be not to cure patients, but to join with them in a struggle, which we do not abandon. Our motto then might be (in Latin) *Ne cedet mali*; yield not to evil.

18

Victim and Perpetrator

John L. Young

As we so willingly involve ourselves in trying to be helpful to the perpetrators of horrible crimes, we may appropriately deal with this deviant aspect of our personalities by acknowledging our natural interest in the victim and following it to gain a fuller understanding of how we can address the needs that victim and perpetrator share.

An American sister has recently written an important book. She is Sister Helen Prejean (Prejean 1993), a sister in the sense of a nun, not a nurse as in the English usage, which arises from the earliest nurses being in fact religious nuns. Quite by accident, Sister Helen began a practice of writing letters to condemned prisoners – in the US where we still condemn some prisoners, unlike in all of your more advanced countries. Through her book she shares her discovery of the importance of meeting the victim history of the perpetrator and tells the story of how she herself confronted it with at least some success.

Not only was she surprised when the prisoners wrote back, but she made discoveries about their victims, which amazed her and became a major thread woven into her book. Naturally enough, she assumed, the families and relatives of victims would want absolutely nothing to do with her. She supplemented her assumption with avoidant rationalizations such as not wanting to rekindle their grief or drain off too much of her own time and energy. Before long, she came to realize that this was a mistake, and her book is essentially a sharing of the journey through her experience of facing the truth of that discovery.

She began by learning that some victims were actually surprised that she had not reached out to them in the beginning. She soon found that many of these family members preferred to be called survivors, a preference that she found somewhat vexing. Dr. Adshead (Chapter 17) has explained this reaction in terms of the universal challenge of facing the stark reality that there was a human perpetrator. Yet, she asserts, this must be done in order to worthily assist the victim.

Although she writes primarily to build a case for the abolition of capital punishment, Sister Prejean's contribution is important, because it confirms and illuminates that we must attend to the challenge of the victim if we are to accomplish as well as possible the work that we can do.

Sister Helen also discovered that far too many victims are neglected by the system, often clearly, because of their race and/or class. The victims to whom Sister Helen ministers have the same important and challenging needs as those with whom Dr. Adshead has worked. At a minimum, they need effective support, while time does her healing work. They need special help at anniversaries of the events that made them victims. And they need sustained help dealing with reactions such as vengeful urges and the resultant feelings of guilt.

Having information about the victim is important in order to assess and treat the perpetrator adequately. This key point is easily overlooked, which is a perilous thing to do. Further, the rage I mentioned earlier may go so far as to make victims become also perpetrators. In addition, I agree strongly with the emphasis on distinguishing the many and quite diverse types of victims.

Pondering the challenge of the victim also leads me to ask a number of questions that some can try to answer from experience. I will ask the boldest one: what if one were to form a treatment group combining victims and perpetrators? And I conclude with strong support for the proposition that we attend to the challenge of the victim as a matter of moral urgency.

19

The Victim in the Offender

Cleo Van Velsen

To begin my chapter, I would like to quote Pavese: 'Every victim resembles every survivor and asks himself why.' This is a central question here today.

Gwen Adshead (Chapter 17) made the point that our wisdom, or knowledge, of the victim is scant: this is important, because it refers to a lack of in depth understanding which is certainly the case. On a superficial level, however, it is a surprising claim as there seem to be victims everywhere one turns – rape victims, war victims, torture victims, AIDS victims, but also fashion victims, media victims, victims of sexual harassment and victims of political correctness about sexual harassment. In our culture at present, there is a jostling to be a victim. It may be a relief to smokers here to know, with regard to new reports, that people who choose to smoke and ruin their health are actually victims of tobacco companies – powerless, impotent individuals at the mercy of forces beyond their control!

Similarly, recently an insurance company in the United States became alarmed at the exponential increase in claims from those injured in accidents in public buses and so they filmed a deliberately set-up bus accident. In the few minutes after the crash seventeen people were seen scrambling *onto* the bus in order to claim injury. Such concerns are well described by Robert Hughes (1993) and his work on the 'culture of complaint', also referred to by Gwen Adshead.

It could be argued that I trivialize the issue, but I think there is a real difficulty in actually knowing what is being seen, heard and described by ourselves and our patients. I also think it important to be wary about the possible over-use of certain terms in our field, and victim is one of them.

The problem about being a victim is that he or she needs to remain so in order to deserve compassion, understanding and indeed compensation. Victimhood also bestows innocence and victims must remain oppressed and underfoot, or risk our fury at having been duped. This can be seen on a cultural level, but is also true for the countertransference in psychoanalytic psychotherapy with victims and offenders.

In the United Kingdom there is an organization called the Child Support Agency, which has recently been founded to collect the millions of pounds of unpaid maintenance from men due to their children, from whom they have been separated for reasons of divorce, etc. A good idea, one might think, but it has unleashed a vicious battle concerning who the real victims are. The men are now saying they are the victims who are being hounded out of house and home and being driven to suicide, and so forth. There is talk of lazy ex-wives who will not work and a virulent hatred for the female head of the Child Support Agency.

Similarly with our offender patients there is often a sense that they have forfeited their right to victimhood by crossing the line into victimizing criminal activity. As Gwen Adshead pointed out, there is here an audience interested in the rather strange creature called forensic psychotherapy which, if it means anything, must mean an understanding of the victim in the offender and *vice versa*. I would suggest that even we as forensic psychotherapists find it difficult not to split into a world of goodies and baddies. An example is the use of confrontation in treatment – surely important.

However, confrontation must be internal to encourage change and this may take some time as well as slow and patient work. All too often 'confrontation' seems to involve pushing something violently into a patient in a way that usually repeats earlier violent experiences and can at times be catastrophic. Similarly, defence mechanisms such as identification with the aggressor can quickly come to mind, but actually be hard to recognize in our patients.

Gwen Adshead equates traumatization and victimization and I wonder if we do not need to be a little careful of that: everyone who is victimized, harmed and wronged, has undergone some kind of trauma, but not all traumas create victims. Freud taught us that our lives are lived by progressing through traumas constantly: expulsion from the womb, loss of the breast by weaning, displacement by a younger sibling, puberty, death of parents, the list could go on and on. Can we say, however, that the death of mother or father makes one a victim – surely this is not automatic, but must depend on circumstance. The arrest, torture, and disappearance of a parent in a repressive state might be one such circumstance. The death of a parent from 'natural' causes is very different. The language of victims and post traumatic stress disorder threatens to hijack concepts and language that we already have and which are of major importance – loss, grief, and mourning. A particular example is the term 'secondary post traumatic stress disorder', used recently in the context of relatives who watched, on TV, people they knew die in the Hillsborough Stadium Disaster and then went to court to claim compensation (which was denied). How useful is such a term in such a context?

As Gwen Adshead highlights, there are times when people are victims through no fault of their own. But I would argue that these are not the ones we, as health professionals, tend to see as they either do not seek help or get in to trouble. Related to this, people who have experienced traumas, especially perhaps disasters, are beginning to complain about the descent into their lives of those offering counselling and treatment.

It is, of course, important to validate certain victimizing experiences which someone has endured. I shall use as an example a group of people with whom I have worked, namely those who have been tortured: this involves physical and psychological maltreatment, but also concomitant losses, i.e. of family, profession, etc. I found it important to be modest about overmedicalizing, diagnosing and treating these people. In my view they often need us to help bear witness to their experiences, and to validate the harm, injustice and suffering that they have undergone. This is a function of one's job as a doctor, psychiatrist and other health professional, but I would say that we need to be cautious in thinking that it is our job as psychoanalytic psychotherapists.

For the minority I treated with psychoanalytic psychotherapy, it was essential to try and stick to the boundaries of known technique and modify only after careful thought and discussion.

Grievance and vengefulness, also, are interesting and important phenomena to be alive to in our work with victims, although I do not here have time to develop it in much depth. Examples include certain therapeutic groups for women who have been victims of sexual abuse. A group such as this can become a paranoid arena for constant rehearsal of the abuse in a way that does not necessarily help any working through as it is more of an action than a symbolic communication. Instead there is a joining together of the group members in a hatred of every man and a massive sense of grievance. This might be understandable, and even helpful, for a short time, but I think that it can lead to the fate of being a victim for ever.

I am not stating that a psychotherapist can claim moral neutrality, but I think it is perhaps a goal to aim for. It certainly does not mean amorality and collusion with an offender. The massive task with offenders is to enable them to know themselves about the damage they have done and do, and to see if any reparation or change is possible. They have often had years of people telling them what they do is unacceptable with little effect. In the context of treatment, the mobilization of a harsh and primitive super-ego must be done with sensitivity. Sometimes, perhaps often, change may not be possible: the persecutory and annihilatory and depressive anxieties are too great, and the damage too profound. Both over-zealous therapeutic aims and cynical hopeless despair must be avoided.

With victims I would suggest that there needs to be a place for the exploration of whether or not the trauma keyed in to a psychic reality in a way that has locked the person into their position as victim. Finally I propose that our task as psychotherapists is to acknowledge our own investment in this kind of work, especially the excitement that suffuses the discussion of violence, attack and hurt.

There is still so much to know and learn and I will end with a quote from Empson writing about King Lear, whom he sees as a scapegoat, and you can substitute the word victim for our purpose. He points out something about victims and our relation to them that is subtle, but important.

'The scapegoat who has collected all this wisdom for us is viewed at the end with a sort of hushed envy, not, I think really, because he has become wise, but because the general human desire for experience has been so glutted in him; he has been through everything.' (Hamilton 1988)

References

Akhtar, S. (1992) *Broken Structures Severe Personality Disorders and their Treatment.* Northvale, NJ: Jason Aronson Inc.

Argelander, H. (1976) *The Initial Interview in Psychotherapy*, Translated by Bernays, H.F. New York: Human Sciences Press.

Bachelard, G. (1969) *The Poetics of Space.* Boston: Beacon Press.

Bateson, G. (1979) *Mind and Nature: A Necessary Unity.* London: Wildwood House.

Berg, W. van den (1993) Conference.

Beyaert, F.H.L. (1982) 'Different penal systems and some consequences for forensic psychiatry.' *Uit: J. Lan and Psychiatry 5*, 425–429.

Bion, W. (1959) *Experiences in Groups.* New York: Basic Books.

Bion, W. (1962) *Learning from Experience.* London: Heineman.

Bollas, C. (1987) *The Shadow of the Object; Psychoanalysis of the Unthought Known.* London: Free Association Books.

Bowlby, J. (1988) *A Secure Base.* London: Penguin.

Bremner, D.J., Southwick, S., Johnson, D.R., Yehuda, R. and Charney, D.S. (1993) 'Childhood physical abuse and combatrelated post-traumatic stress disorders.' *American Journal of Psychiatry 150*, 235–239.

Brownmiller, S. (1975) *Against our Will.* London: Penguin.

Bruch, H. (1974) *Learning Psychotherapy; Rationale and Ground Rules.* Cambridge MA: Harvard University Press.

R v Canons Park Mental Health Review Tribunal Ex parte A, [1994] 2 AII ER 659 CA.

Chiswick, D. (1993) Paper, The Mental Health Act 1983: time for change? Conference, Law Society, Mental Health Act Commission and Institute of Psychiatry, London.

Coid, J. (1988a) 'Mentally abnormal remands I: rejected or accepted by the NHS.' *British Medical Journal 296*, 1779–1787.

Coid, J. (1988b) 'Mentally abnormal remands II: comparison of services provided by Oxford and Wessex regions.' *British Medical Journal 296*, 1783–1784.

Coid, J. (1993) Paper, The Mental Health Act 1983: time for change? Conference, Law Society, Mental Health Act Commission and Institute of Psychiatry, London.

Cope, R. (1993) 'A survey of forensic psychiatrists views on psychopathic disorder.' *The Journal of Forensic Psychiatry 4*, 2, 215–235.

Cox, M. (1983) 'The contribution of dynamic psychotherapy to forensic psychiatry and vice versa.' *International Journal of Law and Psychiatry 6*, 89–99.

Cox, M. and Theilgaard, A. (1987, 1997) *Mutative Metaphors in Psychotherapy The Aeolian Mode.* London: Jessica Kingsley Publishers.

Cox, M. and Theilgaard, A. (1994) *Shakespeare as Prompter: The Amending Imagination and the Therapeutic Process.* London: Jessica Kingsley Publishers.

Craft (1965) *Ten Studies of Psychopathic Personality.* Bristol: Wright.

Dahl, H. (1972) 'A quantative study of psychoanalysis.' In R.R. Holt and E. Peterfreund (eds) *Psychoanalysis and Contemporary Science.* New York: Macmillan.

Dahl, H. (1974) 'The measurement of meaning in psychoanalysis by computer analysis of verbal contaxt.' *Journal of the American Psychoanalytic Association 22*, 37–57.

Dahl, H. (1979) *Word Frequencies of Spoken American English.* Essex, CT: Verbatim.

Davie, D. (1964) 'Yeats, the master of a trade.' In Donoghue, D. (ed) *The Integrity of Yeats.* Cork: The Mercier Press.

Department of Health and Social Security/Home Office (1986) Consultative Document on offenders suffering from psychopathic disorder. Review of a proposal for reform of the law. DHSS/Home Office, London.

Dickinson, E. (1970) *The Complete Poems.* London: Faber and Faber.

Dolan, B. and Coid, J. (1993) *Psychopathic and Antisocial Personality Disorders. Treatment and Research Issues.* London: Royal College of Psychiatrists/Gaskell.

Fairbairn, R. (1952) *Psychoanalytic Studies of the Personality.* London: Routledge and Kegan Paul.

Foulkes, S.H. (1964) *Therapeutic Group Analysis.* London: George Allen and Unwin.

Foulkes, S.H. (1990) *On Group – Analytic Psychotherapy in Selected papers of S.H. Foulkes; Psychoanalysis and Group Analysis.* Edited by Foulkes, E. London: Karnac Books.

Fox Keller, E. (1985) *Reflections on Gender and Science.* New Haven, Yale.

Frazer, J. (1922) *The Golden Bough.* London: Macmillan, 1978, p.383.

Freud, S. (1919) 'Turning in the way of psychoanalytic therapy.' In *Collected Papers 2,* 1946, p.400. (trans. Riviere), London: Hogarth.

Gallwey (1991) *Social Management in Textbook of Psychotherapy Practice.* Edited by Jeremy Holmes, Churchill Livingstone.

Gallwey, P. (1992) Personal communication.

Garland, C. (1991) 'Trauma and its impact on the internal world.' In J. Holmes (ed) *Textbook of Psychotherapy in Psychiatric Practice.* London: Churchill Livingstone.

Gelder, M., Gath, D. and Mayou R. (1989) *Oxford Textbook of Psychiatry,* second edition. Oxford: Oxford University Press.

George, C., Kaplan, N. and Main, M. (1985) *The Adult Attachment Interview.* Unpublished manuscripts. University of California at Berkely, Department of Psychology.

Goffman, E. (1961) *Asylums.* Harmondsworth: Pelican Books.

Grawe, K., Donati, R. and Bernaue, F. (1994) Psychotherapie im Wandel, Von der Konfession zur Profession. Göttingen: Hogrefe.

Green, B. (1993) 'Survivors at risk.' In J. Wilson and B. Raphael (eds) *International Handbook of Trauma.* New York: Plenum Press.

Gunderson, J.G. and Kolb, J.E. (1978) 'Discriminating features of the borderline patients.' *American Journal of Psychiatry,* 13–5:7.

Gunn, J. (1992) 'Personality disorders and forensic psychotherapy.' *Criminal Behaviour and Mental Health 2,* 2, 202–211.

Gunn, J. and Taylor, P. (eds) (1993) *Forensic Psychiatry. Clinical, Legal and Ethical Issues.* Butterworth: Heineman.

Hamilton, I. (1988) *Robert Lowell: A Biography.* London: Faber and Faber.

Harding, T. (1992) 'Psychopathic disorder: time for a decent burial of a bad legal concept?' *Criminal Behaviour and Mental Health 2,* 2, vi–ix.

Housman, A.E. (1939) *Collected Poems.* London: Jonathan Cape.

Hughes, R. (1993) *Culture of Complaint.* New York: Oxford University Press.

Kernberg, O.F. (1971) 'Prognostic considerations regarding borderline personality organisation.' *Journal of the American Psychoanalytic Association 19,* 595–635.

Kernberg, O.F. (1984) *Severe Personality Disorders: Psychotherapeutic Strategies.* New York: Jason Aronson Inc.

Lifton, R.J. (1973) *Home from the War,* third edition. (1992). Boston: Beacon Press.

Lord, P. (1957) Report of the Royal Commission on the Law Relating to Mental Illness and Mental Deficiency 1954–1957. Cmd. 169, HMSO, London.

Main, T. (1957) 'The ailment.' *British Journal of Medical Psychology 30,* 129–145.

Main, T. (1989) 'Psychiatrists, psychotherapies and psychoanalytic training.' In T. Main (Johns, J., ed.) *The Ailment and other Psychoanalytic Essays.* London: Free Association Books.

Marle van, H.J.C. (1991) 'Motivatie in de klinisch forensisch psychiatrische behandeling.' In R.V. Schwartz and D.H. Linszen (eds) *Persoonlijkheidsstoornissen, Doagnostiek, Behandeling, Beleid.* Amsterdam: Swets en Zeitlinger B.V.

Marle van, H.J.C. (1993) *De Hang Naar Dwang.* Arnhem, Gouda Quint.

Marle van, H.J.C. (1995) *Het Gesloten Systeem.* Arnhem, Gouda Quint (with a summary in English).

Masterson, J.F. (1976) *Psychotherapy of the Borderline Adult; A Developmental Approach.* New York: Brunner-Mazel.

Mergenthaler, E. and Stinson, C. (1992) 'Psychotherapy transcription standards.' *Psychotherapy Research 2,* 125–142.

Mergenthaler, E. and Kächele, H. (1991) 'University of Ulm: the Ulm Text Bank Research Program.' In L.E. Beutler (ed) *Psychotherapy Research. An International Review of Programmatic Studies.* American Psychological Association. Washington D.C.

Mergenthaler, E. and Kächele, H. (1993) 'Locating text archives for psychotherapy research.' In N.E. Miller, L. Luborsky, J.P. Barber and J.P. Docherty (eds) *Psychodynamic Treatment Research. A Handbook for Clinical Practice.* New York: Basis Books.

Myerson, P.G. (1979) 'Issues of technique where patients relate with difficulty.' *International Review of Psychoanalysis 6*, 363–375.

Pfäfflin, F. (1981) 'Attempted sexual murders. Aims and conditions of treatment.' Paper read at the 7th International Congress on Law and Psychiatry, The Hague, 23–27 September.

Pfäfflin, F. (1992) 'What is in a symptom? A conservative approach in the treatment of sex offenders.' *Journal of Offender Rehabilitation 18*, 5–17.

Prejean, H. (1993) *Dead Man Walking: An Eyewitness Account of the Death Penalty in the United States.* New York: Random House.

Raphael, B. (1986) *When Disaster Strikes.* London: Unwin Hyman.

Rapport, R.N. (1960) *Community as Doctor.* London: Tavistock.

Samuels, A. (1993) *The Political Psyche.* London: Routledge.

Shea, M.T. (1991) 'Standardized approaches to individual psychotherapy of patients with borderline personality disorder.' *Hospital and Community Psychiatry 42*, 10.

Smits, B.G. (1994) 'De therapie-afdeling van het PSC; een behandelingsgevangenis!.' In *Behandelen of straffen? Gestoorden, verslaafden en jeugdigen*, Arnhen: Gouda Quint.

Spence, D.P. (1968) 'The processing of meaning in psychotherapy: Some links with psycholinguistic and information theory.' *Behav Sci 13*, 349–361.

Spence, D.P. (1970) 'Human and computer attempts to decode symptom language.' *Psychosomatic Medicine 32*, 6, 615–625.

Stanko, E. (1990) *Everyday Violence.* London: Pandora.

Stürup, G.R. (1968) *Treating the 'Untreatable': Chronic Criminals at Herstedvester.* Baltimore: The Johns Hopkins University Press.

Torrance, T.F. (1969) *Space, Time and Incarnation.* Oxford: Oxford University Press.

Van Praag, H.M. (1993) *'Make-Believes' in Psychiatry or The Perils of Progress.* New York: Brunner-Mazel.

Welldon, E. (1984) 'The application of group-analytic psychotherapy to those with sexual perversions.' In T. Lear (ed) *Spheres of Group Analysis.* Nass, Co. Kildare: Leinster Leader Ltd.

Welldon, E. (1988) *Mother, Madonna, Whore: The Idealization and Denigration of Motherhood.* New York: Guilford Press.

Welldon, E. (1996) 'Contrasts in male and female perversions.' In C. Cordess and M. Cox (eds) *Forensic Psychotherapy: Crime, Psychodynamics and the Offender Patient.* London: Jessica Kingsley Publishers.

Winnicott, D.W. (1949) 'Hate in countertransference.' *International Journal of Psycho-Analysis 30,* 69–74.

Winnicot, D.W. (1979) 'The theory of the parent–infant relationship.' In *The Maturational Processes and the Facilitating Environment.* London: Hogarth Press.

Wolff, H. (1971) 'The therapeutic and developmental function of psychotherapy.' *British Journal of Medical Psychology 22,* 971–986.

Zulueta de, F. (1993) *From Pain to Violence: The Traumatic Roots of Destructiveness.* London: Whurr.

The Contributors

Adshead, G. Forensic Psychiatrist, Broadmoor Hospital, Crowthorne, UK.

Ballering, I.M. Senior Staff member, Mental Health Policy Division, Ministry of Health, Welfare and Sport, Rijswijk, Netherlands.

Berg van den, W. Legal Counsel, Forensic Observation Clinic, Pieter Baan Centrum, Utrecht, Netherlands.

Cordess, C. Consultant Forensic Psychiatrist, Ealing, and Honorary Senior Lecturer, Charing Cross and Westminster Medical School, London, UK.

Cox, M. Consultant Psychotherapist, Broadmoor Hospital, Crowthorne, and Honorary Research Fellow, The Shakespeare Institute, The University of Birmingham, UK.

Derks, F. Research Psychologist, Dr. H. v.d. Hoeven Kliniek, Utrecht, Netherlands.

Dooley, E. Director of Prison Medical Services, Department of Justice, Dublin, Ireland.

Drost, M. Forensic Psychiatrist, Dr. H. v.d. Hoeven Kliniek, Utrecht, Netherlands.

Du Bois, R. Professor of Adolescent Psychiatry, Tübingen University and Medical Director of Child and Adolescent Psychiatry Unit, Olgahospital, Stuttgart.

Eastman, N.L.G. Barrister at Law and Head, Section of Forensic Psychiatry, St. George's Hospital Medical School, University of London, UK.

Gürişik, Ü. E. Consultant Psychotherapist, Portman Clinic, London, UK.

Marle van, H.J.C. Psychiatrist/Psychotherapist, Professor of Forensic Psychiatry, University of Nijmegen, Medical Superintendent, Pieter Baan Centrum Utrecht, Netherlands.

Pfäfflin, F. Professor of Forensic Psychotherapy, University of Ulm, Ulm, Germany.

Van Velsen, C. Psychotherapist, Maudsley Hospital, London, UK.

Welldon, E. Consultant Psychotherapist, Portman Clinic, Honorary Senior Lecturer, University College, London and Honorary President of the IAFP, London, UK.

West, D.J. Emeritus Professor of Clinical Criminology, University Institute of Criminology, Cambridge, UK.

Wiertsema, H. Managing Director, Dr. H. v.d. Hoeven Kliniek, Utrecht, Netherlands.

Williams, T. Consultant Forensic Psychiatrist, South Wales Forensic Psychiatric Service, Caswell Clinic, Bridgend, Wales, UK.

Young, J.L. Attending Psychiatrist, Associate Professor (Yale), State of Connecticut, Whiting Forensic Institute, Middletown, Connecticut, USA.

Subject Index

Author Index